D1495637

THE ROAD AHEAD FOR THE FED

The Hoover Institution gratefully acknowledges
the generous support of

PRESTON AND CAROLYN BUTCHER

The Road Ahead for the Fed

George P. Shultz
Allan H. Meltzer
Peter R. Fisher
Donald L. Kohn
James D. Hamilton
John B. Taylor
Myron S. Scholes
Darrell Duffie
Andrew Crockett
Michael J. Halloran
Richard J. Herring
John D. Ciorciari

EDITED BY
John D. Ciorciari *and* John B. Taylor

HOOVER INSTITUTION PRESS
Stanford University | Stanford, California

www.hoover.org

Hoover Institution Press Publication No. 574

Hoover Institution at Leland Stanford Junior University,
Stanford, California, 94305-6010

First printing 2009
16 15 14 13 12 11 10 09   9 8 7 6 5 4 3 2 1

Manufactured in the United States of America

The paper used in this publication meets the minimum
Requirements of the American National Standard for
Information Sciences—Permanence of Paper for Printed
Library Materials, ANSI/NISO Z39.48-1992. ∞

Library of Congress Cataloging-in-Publication Data
  The road ahead for the Fed / edited by John D. Ciorciari and
John B. Taylor
    p. cm.
  Includes bibliographical references and index.
  ISBN 978-0-8179-5001-9 (alk. paper)
      1. United States—Economic policy.   2. Federal Reserve banks.
  I. Ciorciari, John D. (John David)   II. Taylor, John B.

  HC106.83.R63   2009
  332.1'10973—dc22
                                                    2009019956

Contents

Introduction   vii
JOHN D. CIORCIARI AND JOHN B. TAYLOR

PART I: DIRECTIONS FROM POLITICS, HISTORY
AND THE MARKET   1

1   Think Long   3
     GEORGE P. SHULTZ

2   Policy Principles: Lessons from the Fed's Past   13
     ALLAN H. MELTZER

3   The Market View: Incentives Matter   33
     PETER R. FISHER

PART II: THE FED'S ENTRY AND EXIT STRATEGIES   49

4   Monetary Policy in the Financial Crisis   51
     DONALD L. KOHN

5   Concerns about the Fed's New Balance Sheet   67
     JAMES D. HAMILTON

6   The Need for a Clear and Credible Exit Strategy   85
     JOHN B. TAYLOR

PART III: PAVING THE WAY WITH MARKET AND REGULATORY REFORMS — 101

7   Market-Based Mechanisms to Reduce Systemic Risk   103
MYRON S. SCHOLES

8   Policy Issues Facing the Market for Credit Derivatives   123
DARRELL DUFFIE

9   Should the Federal Reserve Be a Systemic Stability Regulator?   137
ANDREW CROCKETT

10   Systemic Risks and the Bear Stearns Crisis   151
MICHAEL J. HALLORAN

11   Why and How Resolution Policy Must Be Improved   171
RICHARD J. HERRING

Key Principles and Recommendations   189
JOHN D. CIORCIARI

Acknowledgments   207
About the Authors   211
Index   217

INTRODUCTION

THE FEDERAL RESERVE is the single most important economic policy institution in the United States. This spring the two of us and the ten other authors of this book came together to present and to discuss our views about the future of the Fed. The catalyst for our meeting was the series of unprecedented actions and interventions taken by the Fed relating to the financial crisis. The Fed created new lending facilities for banks and primary dealers, bought part of the Bear Stearns portfolio, infused funds into AIG, purchased assets backed by mortgages, student loans, and credit cards, loaned to foreign central banks, intervened in the commercial paper market, and bought long-term government bonds. By taking these actions the Fed exploded its balance sheet and raised serious concerns in many quarters about inflation, as well as the independence and effectiveness of the Fed.

In this book we and our coauthors address these concerns. We differ in our assessments and our proposals, but we have a common purpose: to understand how the Fed arrived at this unusual juncture, how it can best navigate the road ahead, and how the road itself can be designed to reduce the likelihood of crisis-driven interventions in the future. Moreover, although each author wrote individually, the chapters were put together following our meeting to reflect other views and to integrate them in a logical exposition.

The book is divided into three parts. Part I provides principles and directions for the Fed going forward by drawing on political, historical, and market experiences. Part II presents the central debate over the rationale for the Fed's actions, the seriousness of the dangers, and the exit strategy, with contrasting views from inside and outside the Fed. Part III proposes and examines new market-based mechanisms and regulatory reforms that can help the Fed exit from its exceptional programs and keep it on the road to good monetary policy in the future.

PART I. DIRECTIONS FROM POLITICS, HISTORY, AND THE MARKET

George Shultz opens by urging policy analysts both inside and outside the Fed to "think long" as they address today's challenges facing the U.S. and global economies. Drawing from decades of policy experience, including the years when he was Secretary of the Treasury, he shows how short-term responses to economic challenges can generate unintended and undesirable longer-term consequences.

Allan Meltzer then puts the Fed's response to the current crisis in historical perspective, drawing from his recently-completed history of the Fed. He shows why only a return to proven economic policy principles can restore discipline and stability to the system.

Peter Fisher explains how easy money, unbounded government sponsored enterprises, and excessive leverage led us into the crisis by misaligning incentives. Drawing from his market experience, he urges that the Fed explain clearly its objectives—including which fire it is trying to put out and why—as it charts its future course.

PART II. THE FED'S ENTRY AND EXIT STRATEGIES

Essential to mapping and designing the road ahead is knowing where you are and how got there, which is the objective of this central part of the book. As will be most apparent from the chapters that constitute this part, there is a raging debate about these issues.

Federal Reserve Board Vice-Chairman Donald Kohn opens this part with the view from inside the Fed. He explains the Fed's rationale for its extraordinary actions and draws attention to a number of potential risks that the Fed is attempting to address. He also responds to concerns raised about inflation and Fed independence.

James Hamilton shows, with a dramatic series of charts, the impact of the Fed's actions on the size and composition of the Fed's balance sheet. He explains the hazards, raising concerns about the Fed's role in credit allocation, inflation threats, and the loss of central bank independence. John Taylor follows up on Hamilton's concerns with recommendations on how to execute a clear and credible exit strategy from the exceptional measures taken to date and return to the type of monetary policy that worked well before the crisis began.

PART III. PAVING THE WAY WITH MARKET AND REGULATORY REFORMS

One reason the Fed has taken such unprecedented interventions in this crisis was its worry that the failure of a financial institution which was "too big or too interconnected to fail" would have harmful cascading effects on the economy. If the Fed is to stay on the road of good monetary policy in the future, it will have to say no to requests for bailouts. It will be easier for the Fed to do so if systemic risks are successfully managed through a combination of market-based mechanisms and regulatory reforms.

Myron Scholes leads off with a look at market-based mechanisms. He shows how moving risks from institutions to markets can reduce overall risks in the financial sector and improve its resilience to shocks. He proposes new ways to reduce vulnerabilities stemming from volatility, leverage, and government guarantees. One key to enhancing stability in the financial system will be to strengthen the market for derivatives. Darrell Duffie delves into this important topic. He recommends more market transparency and examines the ways in which a central clearing counterparty can help reduce risk in the markets for credit default swaps and other derivatives.

Can regulatory policy be improved to deal better with risks of a systemic nature given the interconnectedness of the financial system? Andrew Crockett examines the possible usefulness of a systemic stability regulator for this purpose. He reviews the functions that such a regulator could usefully perform and considers the pros and cons of assigning that role to the Fed. Drawing from experience at the SEC during the Bear Stearns crisis, Michael Halloran shows deficiencies in the existing framework for risk regulation and argues that a systemic regulator is needed. Crockett and Halloran agree that the Fed ought not be given this additional responsibility.

Can a new resolution authority for non-bank financial institutions help reduce the need for Fed interventions? Richard Herring argues that it would and examines in detail how such a resolution policy might work in practice. He raises difficult international coordination issues that must be addressed because of the global structure of large financial institutions. To deal with this problem, he recommends that financial firms develop detailed wind-down contingency strategies and submit them for review to their regulatory authorities.

COMMON THEMES WITH REVEALING DEBATES

Common threads connect all the chapters even as differences emerge. All raise concerns about the implications of the Fed's extraordinary actions. There is a strong consensus that there must be an exit, but debate about how difficult such an exit will be. There is agreement about the risks of future inflation, though differences about how and whether the Fed will be able to contain them. There are general concerns about the independence of the Fed in the future, but debate about how difficult it will be to address them. There is agreement that market-based mechanisms and regulatory reforms will help the Fed focus on basic principles of monetary policy in the future, yet a range of views about whether to emphasize markets or government regulatory reform.

In the concluding chapter, John Ciorciari observes that three principles raised in the opening part are repeated throughout the book. We must: (1) consider the long term consequences of short term interventions, (2) put incentive effects front and center in every action and reform, and (3) marry market-based mechanisms with enhanced regulation to achieve optimal outcomes. We believe that these three principles—and the constructive analysis contained in these pages—can serve as guideposts on the road ahead for the Fed.

John D. Ciorciari and John B. Taylor
May 4, 2009

PART I:

DIRECTIONS FROM POLITICS, HISTORY, AND THE MARKET

1

THINK LONG

George P. Shultz

THE EFFORT TO THINK LONG, to think ahead, to consider future consequences, is especially important at a time of crisis when attention is understandably focused on the immediate. Further, I believe that the effectiveness of immediate measures is substantially improved when people can see that long-term issues are being kept in mind and dealt with sensibly. My plan here is to say a few words about one of the problems and one of the possibilities that come to mind when you think long.

History doesn't repeat itself in any precise way, but it is nevertheless worthwhile to take a look back to see what sort of trends and what sort of relationships seem to assert themselves. When you're thinking about the Fed, the best way to start is to consult Volume 1 of Allan Meltzer's magisterial *History of the Federal Reserve,* which takes us up to 1951. (I eagerly await his forthcoming Volume 2.) That was the year of the Accord, and the history of the prior ten years is instructive.

During World War II, the country was mobilized and motivated to win the war. Federal spending and the federal deficit soared. The Federal Reserve had the job of seeing to it that all Treasury issues succeeded at the pegged 2.5 percent rate and that they stayed successful. To put it another way, the Fed helped the Treasury finance the war by creating the money necessary to see that the Treasury could sell its bonds. The inflationary impact was presumably dealt with by very high marginal rates of taxation (over 90 percent) and wage and price controls. So here we see the interplay of inflation, tax rates, and controls as a consequence of persistent high deficits, with the Fed acting as the Treasury's financier.

After the war, the controls were dropped, but the Fed continued its role as maintainer of the 2.5 percent peg. As the economy expanded vigorously, members of the Federal Reserve Board became restive. President Harry Truman felt that it was wrong to let interest rates rise and reduce the value of bonds purchased during the war. Secretary of the Treasury John Snyder apparently thought that changes in interest rates would, in any case, be ineffective in controlling inflation and advocated a return to wage, price, and credit controls. Differences over policy and other issues led to a January 17, 1951, meeting of Chairman of the Fed Thomas McCabe, Secretary of the Treasury Snyder, and President Truman, after which Snyder gave a speech reaffirming the 2.5 percent peg. This was not the position of many Federal Reserve members, and even supporters of the peg grew uncomfortable with the Treasury's overbearance. Feelings apparently ran high. Here is one commentary printed by the *New York Times* and quoted in Meltzer's book:

In the opinion of this writer, last Thursday constituted the first occasion in history on which the head of the Exchequer of a great nation had either the effrontery or the ineptitude, or both, to deliver a public address in which he has so far usurped the function of the central bank as to tell the country what kind of monetary policy it was going to be subjected to. For the moment at least, the fact that the policy enunciated by Mr. Snyder was, as usual, thoroughly unsound and inflationary, was overshadowed by the historical dimensions of his impertinence.

All this led to an unprecedented January 31 meeting of the full Fed Open Market Committee with the president in the White House. Although the outcome of the meeting was apparently ambiguous, the Treasury reported that the "Federal Reserve Board has pledged its support to President Truman to maintain the stability of government securities as long as the emergency lasts," which was later clarified by the Treasury as maintaining the 2.5 percent peg.

As Meltzer explains the tensions of the times, "These efforts to force the system to remain subservient accomplished in a few days what most of the members had been unwilling to consider in the previous five and a half years. The Treasury had lied publicly. In the words of Allan Sproul, president of the Federal Reserve Bank from 1941 to 1956, 'publicity concerning yesterday's meeting with the President . . . doesn't accord with the facts.'"

So acrimony put backbone into the Fed, and William McChesney Martin, then in the Treasury and soon to be chairman of the Fed, took over the Treasury end of the negotiations. The eventual result was the Accord, announced on March 4, 1951.

The Fed would withdraw support for the pegged rate and regain control of an independent monetary policy.

Or at least so it seemed. Little noticed was an apparent agreement—the Even Keel—for the Fed to support the Treasury market for a few weeks before and after any Treasury issue. This apparently soft understanding was firmed up by President Lyndon Johnson when financial pressures once again rose as he confronted the necessity to fund simultaneously the Vietnam War and the Great Society programs.

This bit of history shows, among other things, how difficult it is for the Fed to disengage, to be in fact an independent monetary authority, once the Fed has become thoroughly entangled in Treasury operations.

Enter Richard Nixon, Arthur Burns, and John Connally in a drama in which I had a bit part and a ringside seat. There had been a drumbeat of talk in the latter years of the Johnson administration of guidelines for wage and price changes. Conceptually, this was a clear precursor to wage and price controls. With a colleague at The University of Chicago, Robert Aliber, I put together a conference on the subject of informal controls in the marketplace. We had many great papers and lots of good discussion. Milton Friedman led off on the price of guideposts, and Bob Solow followed with "The Case against the Case against the Guideposts." Gardner Ackley weighed in, as did many others, including Allan Meltzer. In a fascinating comment, Milton Friedman said,

> In my opinion, the most serious logical fallacy underlying the analysis of cost-push inflation in the guideposts is the confusion of nominal magnitudes with real magnitudes—of dollars with real quantities or what a dollar will buy. This fallacy is

very deep and affects a great many current views. The basic fallacy is to suppose that there is a trade-off between inflation and employment; that is, to suppose that, by inflating more over any long period of time, you can have on the average a lower level of unemployment. This is the notion underlying the desire to maintain a great deal of pressure on aggregate demand and, when you want to avoid the symptoms of inflation, to try to suppress them by guideposts, guidelines, and the like.

That was Milton's first written exposition of his famous devastating critique of the Phillips curve, later delivered as his presidential address to the American Economic Association.

Against the background of this work at the university, I found myself, as the director of the newly formed Office of Management and Budget, worried about possible reactions to potential inflation and arguing with my friend, the awesome Arthur Burns. He was a great fan of guideposts. I gave a talk entitled "Steady as You Go," arguing that we had the budget under control and that with sensible monetary policies and a little patience, inflation would recede. (In light of subsequent events, I later coined the phrase, "An economist's lag is a politician's nightmare.") In fact, inflation was starting to drift down from a high of around 6 percent. In came John Connally, the handsome Texas activist who said, "I can sell it round or I can sell it flat." The business community weighed in with its fear of wage-price inflation caused by wage increases demanded by strong unions. Somehow, many business leaders seemed to feel that they could have wage controls without price controls. Can you believe that? Only when you hear it yourself.

Along came the collapse of a main pillar of the Bretton Woods system, as the United States could not maintain the promise to exchange gold for dollars at $35 an ounce. With a run on Fort Knox in prospect, the gold window was closed, which had inflationary implications, though overrated since our imports at that time were only 5.4 percent of GDP. The Democratic Congress had passed legislation authorizing— practically daring—President Richard Nixon to impose wage and price controls. Secretary Connally, under those circumstances, easily sold the president on wage and price controls as necessary to deal with the threat of inflation. Once again, as in World War II, the belief was that inflation could be contained by controls, so monetary policy could be eased. And it was, laying the basis for the inflation of the latter part of the 1970s. So once again, we saw the interplay of easy money, inflation, and controls.

With heroic efforts by Paul Volcker as chairman of the Fed operating under the umbrella of Ronald Reagan's political protection, inflation was brought under control by 1982 but with the cost of a tough recession. Reagan ended controls on the price of crude oil immediately on taking office. The marginal rate of taxation was brought down from 70 percent to 50 percent and then, in the bipartisan 1986 Tax Act, to 28 percent. Alan Greenspan, Volcker's successor as chairman of the Fed, effectively reinforced Volcker's heroic efforts. There ensued a quarter century of reasonable economic growth without inflation.

Now here we are again. We have a recession on our hands. Fiscal and monetary policies starting in the last months of the Bush administration and accelerating with the Obama administration have been moving into unprecedented terrain. Federal government spending has moved from a recent history of around 20 percent of GDP to an estimated 28.5 percent in fiscal 2009. The deficit, even as optimistically forecast by the administration in the out-years, is in unsustainable territory, and federal spending remains well in excess of the historic 20 percent level. The Federal Reserve has brought the federal funds rate down to zero and has been extending credit in unprecedented ways. By this time, the Fed has expanded the monetary base by 80 percent in the last six months, an astronomical yearly rate of increase. And its portfolio is increasingly made up of privately generated assets, acquired because their unknown and questionable value made them a drag on the operations of the private organizations that generated them in the first place.

On February 10, Secretary of the Treasury Timothy Geithner announced that

> Working jointly with the Federal Reserve, we are prepared to commit up to a trillion dollars to support a Consumer and Business Lending Initiative. This initiative will kick start the secondary lending markets to bring down borrowing costs and to help get credit flowing again . . .This lending program will be built on the Federal Reserve's Term Asset Backed Securities Loan Facility, announced last November, with capital from the Treasury and financing from the Federal Reserve.

This looks like a Treasury initiative to commit the Fed to a trillion dollars of federal spending, or perhaps the Treasury will put up one-tenth of the money from the Troubled Asset Relief Program.

The authorities seem to be a little uneasy about their

legal authority; in a press release on March 3, the Board of Governors of the Federal Reserve System announced that "Treasury and the Federal Reserve will seek legislation to give the Federal Reserve the additional tools it will need to enable it to manage the level of reserves while providing the funding necessary for the TALF and for other key credit-easing programs."

And then comes the announcement on March 18 that the Fed will purchase up to $300 billion in long-term Treasury securities. As observed by Krishna Guha in the March 19 *Financial Times*, "Once this scheme is fully implemented, its [the Fed's] balance sheet could approach $4,000 billion—nearly a third of the size of the U.S. economy. A swollen Fed balance sheet runs the risk that the U.S. central bank may find it difficult to manage down the money supply when the economy turns, raising the possibility of inflation."

Observing this process, the question comes forcefully at you: Has the Accord gone down the drain? And remember how difficult it was for the Fed to disentangle itself from the Treasury in the post-World War II period.

If you're trying to think ahead and worry about consequences, you have to be concerned about the potential for inflation generated by these huge changes in the money supply and the imbalance in the federal budget. Marginal tax rates are now scheduled to rise, as are rates of taxation on dividends and capital gains.

Will controls be in our future? Who knows? We have a start with executive compensation and with prices and pay in the health industry. But I'm struck by a phrase used by my friend Allan Meltzer in a recent phone conversation. He said, "It's a race between the inflation rate, the tax rate, and controls, and all three are going to win."

The purpose of thinking long is, among other things, to identify potential undesirable consequences and focus on the positive possibilities.

So here is one positive possibility. Much has been made for some years now about the potential problems created by the large international imbalances in trade and payments. As is well known, we have seen a period where high-savings countries have maintained their economies by a large surplus of exports over imports. Meanwhile, other economies, principally the United States, have not saved enough to finance their own investments, so savings have come from abroad, with a counterpart of large excesses in imports over exports. The current economic downturn has shown the validity of the worries about these large, insistent imbalances. Suddenly, in particular the countries that have counted on large exports find their economies hard hit when that possibility diminishes.

Right now, household saving rates in the United States are finally on the rise, having recently gotten up to around 5 percent (the feel of the situation suggests that the number is now higher). This is still one-half or so the rate of saving as recently as the early 1980s. At some point, the world will come out of the current gloomy phase; when that happens, I believe it will be desirable to have greater balance in the new picture. When the United States saves enough to finance its own investment, a more or less balanced trade account will result. Obviously, this means major adjustments elsewhere. That, to my way of thinking, should be a principal item of substance on the international agenda. What it implies for the United States is to welcome the rise in the rate of saving and to match it by drawing down the high degree of dissaving now in prospect in the federal budget.

So, once again, the purpose of thinking long is, among other things, to identify potential undesirable consequences and to think about positive possibilities. I have tried to identify one of each. That is my job here. The job of the rest of this book is to figure out how to avoid the undesirable consequences and capitalize on the positive possibilities.

2

POLICY PRINCIPLES: LESSONS FROM THE FED'S PAST

Allan H. Meltzer

EVENTS FOLLOWING THE START OF THE HOUSING, mortgage and credit market crises in summer 2007 opened a new chapter in Federal Reserve history. Never before had it taken responsibility as lender-of-last-resort to the entire financial system, never before had it expanded its balance sheet by hundreds of billions of dollars or more over a short period, and never had it willingly purchased so many illiquid assets that it must hope will become liquid assets as the economy improves. Chairman Ben Bernanke seemed willing to sacrifice much of the independence that Paul Volcker restored in the 1980s. He worked closely with the Treasury and yielded to pressures from the chairs of the House and Senate Banking Committee and others in Congress.

This chapter is adapted from the epilogue in *A History of the Federal Reserve, Volume 2, Book 1*, forthcoming from the University of Chicago Press.

Events highlighted several flaws in Federal Reserve policy. Current pressures dominated longer-term objectives. The Board had never developed or enunciated a lender-of-last-resort policy. Markets had to observe its actions and interpret the statements as always in the past. Instead of reducing uncertainty by offering and following an explicit lending policy rule, it continued to prevent some failures while permitting others. It failed to give a believable explanation of its reasons and reasoning.

One of the main failings of monetary policy in 1970s was the neglect of longer-term consequences of near-time actions. Whenever the unemployment rate rose to about 7 percent, the members abandoned any concern about the inflationary consequences of their actions. Preventing inflation had to wait. When the right time came, it didn't remain long enough to end inflation. Raising interest rates and slowing money growth raised the unemployment rate, so policy became expansive again. The result: inflation and unemployment both rose.

We seem likely to repeat these mistaken actions. In 2008, the Federal Reserve increased its balance sheet from about $800 billion to more than $2.2 trillion. Many of the assets it acquired are illiquid. The market's demand for reserves rose because they were frightened, uncertain, and lacked confidence that financial fragility and failure would end. Once confidence begins to return, the Federal Reserve will have to absorb large volume of reserves. The 1970s problem will return as an exaggerated problem.

Economists and central bankers have discussed policy discretion for many years. Discretion enabled the Federal Reserve to make the many mistakes discussed in this volume and to facilitate the risky loans that are the source of credit and economic problems after August 2007. The main lesson of these experiences should be that monetary policy should remain consistent with a rule, not a rigid rule but rule-like behavior that responds to both short-term fluctuations in output or employment while maintaining low inflation. Discretion has made too many errors.

In 2008 Congress approved $700 billion for the Treasury to use to support banks and financial institutions. The Treasury lacked a coherent plan and frequently allowed its actions to differ from its statement, adding to uncertainty and lack of confidence in policy. By year end the Treasury had helped 206 banks, and the Federal Reserve had lent $100 billion to support a large failed insurance company. At year-end, President Bush advanced loans to prevent bankruptcy by General Motors and Chrysler, and the Federal Reserve accepted General Motors Acceptance Corporation (GMAC) as a bank so that GMAC could borrow at the discount rate. GMAC immediately offered zero percent interest rate loans to borrowers with less than median credit ratings, precisely the type of loans that caused the crisis.

Financial problems spread to many other countries. Asset owners ran to the dollar and U.S. Treasury securities for safety. This pushed Treasury bill rates to zero or slightly above and lowered longer-term rates. Managing the reversal of these flows will be a major challenge for the Federal Reserve in the future.

Current housing and credit market problems gave rise to expected new claims blaming financial deregulation and hailing the end of American-style capitalism or, in more extreme instances, the end of capitalism. It is hard to ignore such comments, but it is just as hard not to laugh. Despite active criticism and frequent condemnation, capitalism in one form or another has become the dominant form of economic organization throughout the world because only capitalism provides freedom, improved living standards, and an ability to adapt to cultural and institutional differences.

Those who blame recent deregulation are careful not to cite examples. The most recent major change in 1999 repealed the Glass-Steagall prohibition of combined investment and commercial banking. No other country adopted that rule or had a crisis caused by failure to do so. Many years ago, George Benston (1990) showed that at the time proponents did not make a substantive case when they claimed that combined investment and commercial banking was a cause of the Great Depression.

Members of Congress, as usual, looked for scapegoats whom they could blame for financial failures. Others proposed new regulations to increase governmental control of financial firms. Most proposals of this kind presuppose the reason for the financial failures. In this essay, I discuss seven sources of current problems and how systemic problems can be reduced. Bear in mind that most financial firms borrow short to lend long. That arrangement means that crises will occur when there are sudden changes in the economic environment or expectations. All crises cannot be avoided. Risks will remain, but they can be reduced.

SEVEN CAUSES

Repairing the weaknesses of the U.S. financial system that contributed to the crises requires changes in the practices of the Congress, the Administration, the Federal Reserve, and managers of financial institutions. To succeed, changes must recognize the incentives they create. This section discusses principal problems that contributed to make the crisis severe. It suggests changes to reduce risk and uncertainty.

Congress and the Administration

Home ownership has long been regarded as a source of social stability, a public good that Congress and administrations of both parties encourage. Intervention takes several forms. Mortgage interest has remained tax deductible through several tax reforms including 1986 when most other interest payments lost that benefit. The Community Reinvestment Act (1977) encouraged home ownership by lower income groups. The Act gave opportunity for citizen groups to pressure banks to increase inner city lending by rating banks according to how much credit they supplied to low income borrowers. The ratings influenced decisions to permit mergers and branches. In 1995, Congress strengthened the Act. The American Dream Downpayment Act (2003) subsidized credit for low income groups. When that act passed, President Bush said that it was in the national interest to have more people own their home. He neglected to add "if they invested in them." Beginning in 1999, the Federal Housing Administration (FHA) developed the down payment assistance program that permitted no down payment loans.

In 1931, Congress urged the Federal Reserve to help the mortgage and housing markets by buying mortgages. The Federal Reserve declined, saying that was not its responsibility. Congress then established the Home Loan Bank System and followed with other agencies to support housing and the mortgage market. The Federal National Mortgage Association

(FNMA) opened in 1937. Its mandate was to increase liquidity of the mortgage market by buying mortgages. It expanded in the 1960s and became a privately held entity in the late 1960s. The market treated its debt as subject to a full faith and credit federal government guarantee, although the guarantee did not become explicit until the Treasury replaced the management and took control in 2007. The Home Loan Banks chartered Freddie Mac to operate like FNMA. It, too, lacked explicit guarantee of its debt until the Treasury assumed control. In addition, the Government National Mortgage Association (GNMA) is a government corporation that guarantees mortgage securities backed by federally insured or guaranteed loans issued by government agencies such as the FHA and other agencies. Unlike FNMA and Freddie Mac, GNMA does not own mortgages or mortgage-backed securities. Its guarantee subsidizes homeownership by lowering the interest rate on the mortgage.

With all the subsidies and assistance, expansion of mortgages and housing should not surprise anyone. Between 1980 and 2007, the volume of mortgages backed or supported by the three government-chartered agencies rose from $200 million to $4 trillion, an unsustainable compound growth rate of 36 percent a year. As the volume rose, the quality of mortgages declined. Government encouraged this development; in 2005 the Department of Housing and Urban Development introduced a zero down payment loan, as noted above. Lenders expanded subprime mortgages, mortgages to buyers with relatively poor credit histories. Soon after mortgage lenders began to offer mortgages that did not require a down payment. Then they eliminated credit checks on some mortgages. Such mortgages are called Alt-A.

Purchases and support for these sub-prime and Alt-A mortgages put FNMA and Freddie Mac at much greater risk than in the past. In December 2008 Congressional testimony, the heads of three agencies explained that they were aware of the increased risk but believed it necessary to compete with the private market. They did not add that the Federal Home Loan Banks supplied almost half the funding for two large private lenders, Countrywide and Indy Mac, that later failed. Nor did they add that FNMA and Freddie Mac owned one-half the outstanding sub-prime and Alt-A mortgage-related assets. Prodded by members of Congress and the Clinton and Bush administrations, they lowered the quality of their portfolios to promote home ownership. With the failure of FNMA, Freddie Mac, Countrywide, and Indy Mac, taxpayers will bear a considerable loss.

Edmund Gramlich, a member of the Federal Reserve's Board of Governors, warned about the deterioration of loan quality, but he never presented his case to the Board for action. William Poole, President of the Federal Reserve Bank of St. Louis, did the same and spoke publicly about the taxpayer's risk. Alan Greenspan warned Congress about the growth of FNMA and Freddie Mac. There were many other warnings, including from Senator Richard Shelby, a member of the Banking Committee. Congress declined to act and several members denied that there was a problem. Congressional inaction increased the incentive for FNMA and Freddie Mac to accept very risky loans.

There are homebuilders, mortgage lenders, and real estate agents in every Congressional district. This alone encourages support for mortgage and housing subsidies and delays corrective action. It is very likely that the government will continue to subsidize homeownerships. Reform should seek to put the subsidy on the budget and subject it to the appropriation process. Government mortgage market operations were a means of hiding the subsidy and often denying it. The subsidy took the form of a reduced interest rate on FNMA and Freddie Mac borrowing. Provision of the subsidy did not require off-budget finance.

FNMA and Freddie Mac are in receivership and under government control. They should be liquidated and terminated. Congress should vote the subsidy directly.

After much hesitation and policy change, the Treasury used most of the money in the first half of the Troubled Asset Relief Program (TARP) to supply capital to banks and other financial institutions. No large bank was allowed to fail. Once the banks received this assistance, many in Congress wanted to influence the banks' lending. Congress urged them to lend even if it meant acquiring risky loans with sub-standard repayment prospects.

A better alternative would have required bankers to borrow part, perhaps one-half, of the additional capital in the market. That would have increased a bank's cost, and diluted ownership, but it would deter some banks from borrowing from TARP and identify banks that the market considered insolvent. Those banks should fail. Failure means that shareholders lose their investment and management loses its job. The reorganized bank should be sold or merged.

The government and Federal Reserve treat all large banks as "too big to fail." That encourages gigantism. Instead, policy should impose a different standard: if a bank is too big to fail, it is too big. The new standard would increase the incentive for bankers to be prudent.

Role of the Federal Reserve

Many politicians, bankers, and journalists blamed the housing and mortgage crisis on the Federal Reserve. The basis of their complaint was that from 2003 to early 2005 the Federal Reserve held the federal funds rate at one percent. This permitted credit expansion, much of which concentrated in the mortgage market. By the end of 2005, the funds rate reached 5 percent.

During these years, Chairman Alan Greenspan believed and said that the country faced risk of deflation. That was a mistake. Deflation is very unlikely to occur in a country with a relatively large budget deficit, a long-term depreciating currency, and positive money growth. Critics are correct about this part of their criticism. Federal Reserve policy was too expansive as judged by the Taylor rule or the Federal funds rate during the time the real short-term interest rate remained negative in an expanding economy.

The next part is wrong. The Federal Reserve did not force or urge bankers and others to buy mortgage debt. That was the bankers' decision. Prudent bankers avoided excessive accumulation of low quality mortgages. Bankers could have purchased Treasury bills or other assets with lower risk. They decided to overinvest in very risky assets and to lower quality standards. They share responsibility and have the largest share.

One plausible explanation of the errors that many made was the so-called "Greenspan put." Whether such a put was available, the belief was widespread that the Federal Reserve would prevent large losses especially for large banks. Several bankers and investment bankers raised the leverage they accepted and invested in risky assets. Whether or not there was a Greenspan put, prior actions that prevented financial failures, for example protecting Long-Term Capital Management (LTCM), created moral hazard and reduced concerns for risk. Arranging the rescue of LTCM is the most recent example in a long history of preventing failures. Notable examples include First Pennsylvania Bank, Continental Illinois, and most of the New York money market banks during the Latin American debt crisis. Bankers had reason to believe that the Federal Reserve would prevent failures.

One of the criticisms in my *History of the Federal Reserve* is that the Federal Reserve has not announced its lender-of-last-resort strategy in its 95-year history. Sometimes institutions fail, sometimes the Federal Reserve supports them, and sometimes it arranges a takeover by others. There is no clear policy, no policy that one can discern. But there was a firm belief that failure was unlikely at large banks.

The absence of a policy has three unfortunate consequences. First, uncertainty increases. No one can know what will be done. Second, troubled firms have a stronger incentive to seek a political solution. They ask Congress or the administration for support or to pressure the Federal Reserve or other agencies to save them from failure. Third, repeated rescues encourage banks to take greater risk and increase leverage. This is the well-known moral hazard problem.

As financial problems spread in 2008, pressure built on Bear Stearns. The Treasury and the Federal Reserve arranged a takeover. The Federal Reserve contributed by buying—not lending—$29 billion of risky assets. Markets improved. Many bankers claimed the worst was over. A few months later Lehman Brothers failed. Without prior warning, the Federal Reserve and the Treasury announced that they would not prevent the failure. Next the Federal Reserve prevented the bankruptcy of American International Group by replacing management and providing up to $80 billion in credit.

What conclusion could a portfolio manager draw? There was no clear pattern, no consistency in the decisions. Uncertainty increased. Portfolio managers all over the world rushed for the safety of Treasury bills. A classic panic of the kind described by Walter Bagehot followed. Officials did not announce or follow a clear strategy, as Bagehot urged. Regulators reacted to each subsequent rush for safety by guaranteeing in turn bank deposits, money market funds, commercial paper and other instruments.

Influenced by Bagehot's (1873) criticism, the Bank of England announced the lender-of-last-resort policy that it had followed in past crises and successfully followed the policy into the twentieth century. Panics and failures occurred, but they did not spread or accumulate. The policy called for lending without hesitation in a crisis at a penalty rate against acceptable, marketable collateral. That policy induced prudent bankers to hold collateral and it reduced uncertainty.

By guaranteeing deposits, money market liabilities, and other instruments, the Federal Reserve prevented bank runs and further breakdown of the payments system. Unlike the Great Depression depositors could not demand gold from banks but they could demand currency and use deposits to buy gold or Treasury bills with the same effect. Because banks and other financial firms were unwilling to lend to other firms, they too bought Treasury bills and held idle reserves. The Treasury and the Federal Reserve supported these demands by paying interest on idle reserves and by exchanging Treasury bills for less liquid assets.

The Federal Reserve acted creatively to establish new lending facilities to accommodate market demands. They put off to the future any consideration of how and when they can reverse these expansive actions.

One lesson from the current crisis is that the Federal Reserve should announce a lender-of-last-resort strategy and follow it without exception. A second lesson is that Congress should dispense with "too big to fail." Banks and financial firms should not have incentives to become so large that they cannot fail. Too big to fail encourages excessive risk taking and imposes costs on the taxpayers. If banks considered too big to fail are not reduced in size, they should have substantially higher capital requirements including subordinated debt. The very high leverage ratios at large financial institutions responded to the incentives created by earlier rescues and belief in a Greenspan put.

One of the Treasury's proposed reforms gives the Federal Reserve responsibility for maintaining financial stability. This is a poor choice. The Federal Reserve did nothing about growing savings and loan failures in the 1980s. Ending that crisis cost the taxpayers about $150 billion. The Federal Reserve worked with the International Monetary Fund to protect lending banks during the Latin American debt crisis. The crisis began to end when Citicorp's chairman decided to recognize the losses by writing down the debt's value. Others followed. Soon afterward, the Treasury began a systematic program to write down the debt. The Federal Reserve did nothing.

Although Alan Greenspan warned publicly in 1996 about irrational exuberance in the equities market, neither the Federal Reserve nor the Securities and Exchange Commission tried to prevent rampant stock market speculation. And it followed by doing nothing to prevent the large expansion of sub-prime, Alt-A and other mortgage loans and the rise in housing prices. This error will cost taxpayers much more than the savings and loan failures.

Reading transcripts of Federal Open Market Committee meetings, one finds very little discussion of regulatory and supervisory credit problems. The Federal Reserve's record does not support a proposal to increase its responsibility for financial stability. More important, regulation of this kind can only succeed if the regulator makes better judgments about risk than those whose wealth is at risk. A better change would make risk takers bear the risks they take. Failure should remove management and cost stock holders, as in the FDICIA rule (discussed below). Companies would not disappear. They would get new management and stockholders.

FDICIA
In 1991, Congress passed the Federal Deposit Insurance Improvement Act (FDICIA). A main reason for the act was to reduce Federal Reserve lending to failing banks, thereby reducing losses paid by the FDIC. FDICIA gave regulators authority to intervene in solvent banks when losses reduced capital below required limits and to assume control before a bank's capital was entirely gone. The bank could then be sold or merged. Stockholders would take the loss and managers would be replaced. The regulators did not apply FDICIA standards to failing financial firms in this crisis. FDICIA should be extended to apply to all financial institutions. It is an explicit rule that, if enforced, is known to all interested parties. Prudent bankers will act to avoid failure and the loss of their jobs.

Regulation

The financial crisis brought many demands for increased regulation. Few recognize that regulation works best if it takes account of the incentives it fosters. The Basel Accords agreed to by developed countries are a timely example. The Accords required banks to hold more capital if they acquired more risk. The rationale seems clear and unassailable. The practice was very different.

Instead of increasing capital, banks chartered new entities to hold the risky assets. The intent was to keep the risk off their balance sheets. When the mortgage crisis occurred, the banks had to assume the risk and responsibility for losses. Regulation failed, and so did circumvention. The cost to the public is very large. This experience shows again that lawyers and bureaucrats choose regulations, but markets circumvent costly regulations.

Successful regulation recognizes that it creates incentives for avoidance or circumvention. Successful regulation aligns the interests of the regulated with socially desirable outcomes. Successful regulation induces market action to eliminate externalities. Successful regulation recognizes that market participants respond to regulation by changing their actions to find a new optimum.

Regulators rarely respond to this dynamic process by adopting regulations in response to market outcomes. Because all countries have some type of deposit insurance, either de jure or de facto, regulation must limit risk taking. FDICIA provides an incentive to avoid excessive risk. Capital requirements also help to align incentives and avoid excessive risk taking. Regulations such as the Basel Accord do not meet this standard.

After the Treasury supported General Motors and Chrysler

with what will be a growing bailout of automobile companies, the Federal Reserve accepted GMAC as a bank, enabling GMAC to borrow at the discount window. As noted earlier, GMAC at once began to offer zero interest rate loans for up to five years to borrowers with below median credit ratings. This appears to be a response to pressure from prominent members of Congress, a further sacrifice of independence. Many members of Congress want the Federal Reserve to allocate credit to borrowers that they favor. This avoids the legislative and budget process just as Fannie Mae and Freddy Mac did. It subverts the principles of an independent central bank.

Independence is not just important. It is a critical part of the institutionalization of a low inflation policy. It prevents Congress and the administration from financing deficits by printing money. And it avoids pressures for credit allocation to politically favored groups.

Compensation and Incentives

MBAs who graduated from the world's leading business schools purchased and sold mortgages that carried a high degree of risk. In many cases they accepted the credit ratings supplied by others without investigating accuracy. At many banks, traders were well rewarded for doing the transactions and likely fired if they failed to do so. Compensation systems at many firms rewarded short-term increases in revenue without regard for long-term losses. Compensation systems of this kind encourage excessive risk taking.

Not all firms behaved alike. We know now that J.P. Morgan Chase, Bank of America, and some others limited risk taking much more than Citigroup, Merrill Lynch, Bear Stearns, and other failures.

Setting compensation schedules is management's responsibility. Congress cannot establish rules that managements cannot circumvent, if they choose to do so. An improved compensation system would spread rewards over time to permit losses to be recognized. This can be done in many ways. Regulators should encourage and monitor the actions that managements take, but should leave the choice of compensation schedule to management.

Rating Agencies

The mix of incentives facing rating agencies is well-known as a contributor to the credit crisis. The agencies applied a rating system that had worked for decades in rating corporate bonds. This may have misled users. More seriously, rating agencies at times adjusted their ratings to satisfy client demands.

All of the fault does not fall on the rating agencies, but they share the blame. The clients did not look at the underlying securities or question the ratings except to ask for more favorable ratings. They, too, share the blame. Using rating agencies' judgments without due diligence is a mistake.

Rating agencies must develop compensation and incentive programs that reward accuracy of rating achieved over time. The aim is to give the agency and its personnel incentives for diligence and accuracy.

Transparency and Risk

More information improves decisions and reduces risk. But transparency and increased information is most useful when interpretation is clear. Better reporting of asset and liability positions is most useful when risk models permit users to interpret the information correctly.

Risk models contributed to the credit crisis. These models use standard distributions. They make no distinction between permanent or persistent and transitory changes. Deciding whether risk spreads had permanently fallen before the crash or would return toward historic averages played a role in the crisis. Similarly risk models were not useful for deciding whether the increase in house prices, or the decline in 2007, would persist. Improving ability to judge persistence can improve judgments and economic performance.

RECOMMENDATIONS OF THE ISSING COMMITTEE

After the November meeting of the international grouping known as the G-20, the German government appointed a committee chaired by Professor Dr. Otmar Issing to recommend changes in policies, regulations, and supervision that would reduce the chance of future crises. The Issing Committee identified three major causes of incentive misalignment: structured finance, rating agencies, and management compensation. It found that the crisis was a consequence of "massive liquidity and low interest rates" in an "environment of inadequate regulation and important gaps in supervisory oversight [and] inappropriate incentive structures" (Issing 2008, 2). Unlike most comments on regulation, the Issing Committee emphasized incentives. This section summarizes some of its main proposals.

The Committee recommended that the accuracy of rating agencies should be monitored and reported to the public. Rating fees should be linked to the accuracy of past ratings.

Many of the main proposals concern increases in transparency by specifying rules of disclosure that improve incentives by buyers and sellers of financial instruments. Securitization transactions should disclose the allocation of loss to the tranche that receives the first loss. Disclosure should be mandatory to permit the market to price risk more accurately.

The Issing Committee did not propose legal limits on compensation as such rules "are expected to backfire" (ibid., 3). Instead they favored full disclosure and the development by rating agencies and auditors of a metric that reports on management incentives.

The Committee also proposed a global credit register to show exposure by lenders and their counterparties. The report recognized that the register would be incomplete in real time.

CONCLUSION

Instead of looking for scapegoats and evil doers, the credit crisis should be used to recognize and correct errors on several sides. This is a first step to market reforms that reduce the risk of repetition. We cannot avoid all risk and should not try. We can reduce risk by better policy choices.

Public and private actions contributed to the crisis. Congress and several administrations encouraged public agencies to accept much greater risk to promote home ownership. The Federal Reserve failed to develop an effective predictable lender-of-last-resort policy. This failure increased uncertainty. Many banks and financial institutions reward risk taking thereby increasing incentives for actions that later produced losses. Rating agencies erred.

The paper suggests some changes to respond to these failings. Unlike the claim that more regulation is needed, I argue that regulation only works well if it takes account of the incentives it induces. Good regulation aligns public and private interests where there is evidence of market failure. Bad regulation usually requires strong enforcement.

One consequence of the credit and economic crisis is the aggressive response by governments and central banks to restore stability and growth. Eventually the excessive liquidity they created must be eliminated, a task which will not be easily accomplished. The Federal Reserve has not given much thought to how it will avoid inflation after the recovery is underway. And the greatly expanded role of governments and central banks must not become a precedent. A main lesson of this crisis is that societies must reinvent individual responsibility for avoiding excessive risk. This will be neither easy nor popular with many, but the survival and prosperity of a free society requires greater acceptance of individual responsibility for mistakes. We cannot expect a private system to survive if the profits go to the bankers and the losses go to the taxpayers.

We cannot know what will be the future consequence of the crisis and the policy response. We should recognize, however, that despite the severity of the crisis, regulators have not announced a policy or encouraged financial markets to believe that they have abandoned "too big to fail." In fact, mergers have made the largest firms larger.

The broader lesson of this experience should be that policy misjudgments by Congress and the Federal Reserve helped to bring on the crisis. Discretionary policy failed in 1929–33, in 1965–80, and now. The Federal Reserve should announce and follow a rule for its lender-of-last-resort actions. For monetary policy the lesson should be less discretion and more rule-like behavior. For several years, I have proposed a multilateral arrangement under which major currencies—the dollar, the euro, and the yen—would agree to maintain a common low rate of inflation, say 1 to 2 percent. That would work to increase both expected price stability and greater nominal exchange rate stability. To implement the policy, the Federal Reserve should commit to the Taylor rule. For the monetary policy to work well, the Congress and the Treasury should agree to limit the budget deficit to a narrow range. A rule of this kind increases stability of both domestic and global economies. And Congress should put its housing subsidies on budget and close FNMA and Freddie Mac. As the Issing Committee showed, the route to less risky financial markets starts with stabilizing incentives.

BIBLIOGRAPHY

Bagehot, Walter, (1873). *Lombard Street.* Reprint. Homewood, IL: Richard D. Irwin, 1962.

Benston, George, (1990). *The Separation of Investment and Commercial Banking.* London: Macmillan.

Issing, Otmar, (2008). "New Financial Order, Recommendations by the Issing Committee." Washington, DC: G-20, November 15.

3

THE MARKET VIEW: INCENTIVES MATTER

Peter R. Fisher

WHAT WENT WRONG to cause the excessive growth of leverage and credit that led to this particular systemic failure of housing finance and banking? What have been the policy responses to the financial crisis so far? What will be the consequences of the Federal Reserve's extraordinary balance sheet policies?

The principal lesson from a market perspective is that incentives matter. The explicit and implicit rules of the financial system create incentives that guide the behavior of financial agents. By shaping expectations, the intended and unintended impact of policy makers' words, acts, and omissions also create incentives. This suggests a second lesson that policies which may seem sound in concept can still create unintended bad outcomes when implemented without careful consideration of their incentive effects. This chapter will explore the types of market incentives that contributed to the crisis and that the Fed needs to consider as it formulates and implements policies going forward.

What went wrong to cause the excessive growth of leverage and credit that led to this particular systemic failure of housing finance and banking?

Monetary policy was too easy in the United States and in other countries. The savings glut hypothesis begs the question of where the glut of (Asian and especially Chinese) savings came from. It came from a persistent "glut" of (Western and especially American) consumption in excess of income that could have been curtailed but, instead, grew when monetary policy remained too easy for too long. We over-stimulated housing and banking—the most interest-rate sensitive sectors of our economy—even as some other countries did the same thing.

Other factors influenced the outcome because they shaped the contours of the landscape that channeled the surge of credit caused by the prolonged period of monetary accommodation. While there are many agency problems and shortcomings of our financial system that can be accentuated by easy monetary conditions, four stand out as contributing causes of the crisis. They also stand out as an agenda for reducing systemic risk through changes in the rules that guide behavior that should be addressed before we create either a new federal systemic risk regulator or a new federal resolution authority for non-bank financial firms.

A lopsided regulatory process. Our risk-based capital regime for banks has rested on a faulty foundation. After a quarter century of developing ever-more complex risk-based capital rules, it turns out that if you lend money to someone who cannot pay you back, it does not matter whether you hold six, eight, or ten percent capital against that loan because you will end up with losses and be undercapitalized in any event. Somewhere along the way, we seem to have forgotten the core rationale for government intervention in the management of banks: namely, that in competitive markets lenders will tend to chase the apparently wider net-interest margins on loans to riskier borrowers without properly accounting for the probability of default and, thereby, embed instability in their own balance sheets. They are particularly prone to do this in extended periods of monetary accommodation.

Disciplined credit underwriting and crude capital rules will produce a sounder banking system than sophisticated, risk-based (and even counter-cyclical) capital rules applied to credit written with shoddy underwriting. The failure of bank management and bank supervisors to apply *equal or greater* resources to the enforcement of credit standards, as were applied to the design and implementation of capital rules, created a lopsided regulatory process that is inherently unstable. In the absence of greater underwriting discipline, higher capital requirements will make our banking system less efficient but will not make it more stable.

GSEs unbounded. The panoply of federal incentives for housing played an important role in the extended rise of house prices that became a bubble. But particular attention should be paid to the change in the balance sheets of Fannie Mae and Freddie Mac that was permitted after 1993, when the Treasury Department terminated its "traffic cop" role in regulating their debt issuance. The subsequent rapid growth of their balance sheets fueled the housing boom of the 1990s and stimulated the growth of the securitization markets. More importantly, it created an expectation of ever-rising GSE earnings that fatefully led them in this decade, egged on by Congress, to chase wider margins by moving down in credit quality.

What was rationalized as a counter-cyclical force in housing finance became a pro-cyclical one—an important lesson for those now considering new, discretionary counter-cyclical policies to stabilize the financial system. Any future federal support for housing should avoid the perverse combination of private gain and implicit federal guarantees. Once Fannie Mae's and Freddie Mac's balance sheets have been placed in run-off, their mortgage guarantee functions should be merged into a single federal mortgage insurer that only guarantees fixed-rate mortgages.

Credit default swaps and the mispricing of risk. Credit default swaps, which began as a form of credit insurance against the risk of default, mutated from their origins into a form of off-track betting on credit which became a source of instability by accentuating and prolonging the credit cycle. Contrary to conventional wisdom, credit default swaps are not like equity options, because neither the CDS contract nor the underlying bonds trade with anything like the transparent and continuous price discovery that occurs in equity markets. In the absence of exchange-like market depth and transparency, it is an illusion to think that the system as a whole can dynamically hedge recovery values, even though some individual firms may be able to do so and many can enjoy short-term profits from the volatility and lack of price transparency.

The CDS market contributed to the notorious mispricing of risk from 2003 to 2007, as writers of protection (like AIG and the mono-line insurers) became the "greater fools" who mispriced their insurance premiums and ended up owning a disproportionate share of the risk without either adequate reserves or the ability to hedge those risks once the probability of default began to rise.[1]

Now that credit risk has been re-priced, and given the much higher leverage and lower effective cost of carrying credit risk in the CDS market compared with the cash bond market, we can see the re-insurance-like capital and premium cycle now embedded inside of credit. Just as during the upswing credit risk was mispriced too low, as writers of CDS failed to charge adequate premiums and drove down borrowing costs, now in the downswing borrowing costs are being pushed up as borrowers (whose liabilities underlie CDS) are forced to bear the insurance writers' cost of capital. There has also been a failure to disperse risk, in part, because we permitted the major credit intermediaries to write CDS without recognizing the concentration of risk this entails.

The CDS market should be bifurcated. Those names that can trade both the CDS and the underlying bond on an exchange should do so. Those contracts that are bespoke or idiosyncratic and lack sufficient demand so that they cannot be listed on an exchange should be regulated in a manner consistent with an insurance product with adequate reserves held against potential future exposure.

Counterparty exposures and too-big-to-fail. The effective treatment of counterparty trading exposures as super senior creditors under the U.S. Bankruptcy Code amendments of 2005 trans-

---

1. Creating a central counterparty to turn bilateral counterparty exposures into multilateral net exposures is an insufficient answer to these problems. Neither the writers of protection, nor a central counterparty, will be able to protect and hedge themselves effectively in the absence of continuous and transparent price discovery in *both* the CDS contract and the underlying bond.

formed the "too-big-to-fail" problem of our largest deposit takers into the "too-interconnected-to-fail" problem of all major financial firms. Some have claimed that we should be able to ignore intra-financial sector exposures, as not relevant to the resolution of the crisis, because they can net out without an impact on non-financial borrowers. This fails to understand the dynamic that unfolded throughout 2008 and that, to a great extent, these exposures have driven the authorities' behavior.

Trading exposures on all manner of forward contracts—whether CDS, commodity and securities contracts, or repurchase agreements—which fall within a broad definition of "qualifying financial contracts" of virtually all major financial market participants, take precedence over other claims on an intermediary's capital, effectively in advance of bankruptcy.[2] To avoid the uncertainty of a bankruptcy trustee "cherry picking" among individual trades and, thereby, unraveling gross counterparty exposures, it makes sense to permit the netting or offset of all due-to and due-from claims prior the enforcement of the automatic stay that freezes the positions of all creditors. But it does not make sense to permit these net counterparty positions to be enforceable ahead of all other creditors which effectively moves trading exposures to the top of the capital structure.

With this protection, financial firms have had a powerful incentive to convert credit or any exposure into a trading position, and to run-up and concentrate ever-larger exposures to one an-

---

2. This is a consequence of the "clarification" of the treatment of netting arrangements in bankruptcy contained in the Bankruptcy Abuse Prevention and Consumer Protection Act of 2005 amending various provisions of the U.S. Bankruptcy Code, 11 U.S.C. §§ 101-1532.

other. These same exposures became the self-fulfilling rationale for the authorities to feel the need to bail out firms so as to avoid the shock of having capital drained away to support counterparty exposures. What was originally intended to give greater legal certainty to intrafinancial sector exposures to make the financial system more stable perversely became an engine that destabilized the system and increased both the scale and complexity of the too-big-to-fail problem.

To get the incentives aligned to promote the stability of the financial system, we should revise the Bankruptcy Code to make net counterparty exposures subordinated to other creditors. This would create strong incentives for firms to demand bilateral margin or move trading activity into clearinghouses and exchanges. This would more effectively reduce systemic risk than either increased capital charges for counterparty exposures or the creation of a new federal resolution authority (which oddly aims to make the financial system more stable by making its capital structure less predictable). By encouraging collateralization of trading exposures, such a change would make it easier for firms to be placed in bankruptcy rather than be bailed out.

What have been the policy responses
to the financial crisis so far?

Having pumped up financial balance sheets, the crisis has involved a reversal of this process. As the liabilities of banks and near-banks represent forms of money and near-money, shrinking the balance sheets of financial intermediaries is hard to do without destroying some forms of stored wealth. Policy makers have sought to de-lever the highly-levered balance sheet of our banking system with as little spillover as possible to confidence, consumption, and income. Since August of 2007, the authorities have pursued four distinct strategies that roughly correspond with the phases of the crisis.

Slow it down. To ease the de-levering process, but also to respond to the anticipated decline in aggregate demand, the Federal Reserve's initial response was to lower policy rates and to begin a liberalization of collateralized lending facilities. Over time, this liberalization came to include longer terms, alternative pricing mechanisms, a wider pool of eligible collateral, provision of dollars to foreign central banks to on-lend (through central bank swap lines) and, ultimately, additional counterparties. Lower rates and expanded liquidity facilities undoubtedly offset somewhat the tightening of financial conditions. But if the problem is too much leverage, you can temporarily ameliorate but cannot solve this problem with more lending. You cannot de-lever by borrowing money, even from the central bank.

Speed it up. At year-end 2007 several major financial firms took significant write downs and raised new equity. In early March Federal Reserve officials publicly urged banks to take losses promptly on their mortgage exposures (Bernanke 2008) and to raise new equity capital (Geithner 2008). Recognition of lower principal values could have the effect of stabilizing both home prices and mortgage asset values at higher levels than might be achieved later to the benefit of both borrower and lender. The injection of new equity into banks could achieve a de-levering of balance sheets and also help absorb losses. Such an approach could have helped the de-levering process.

But the public foreshadowing of the process, by officials responsible for bank supervision, had the regrettably perverse effect of threatening existing bank shareholders with an acceleration of losses and a dilution of their ownership interests, the anticipation of the event being quite a different thing from the announcement of a *fait accompli*. The pronouncements by policy makers created a powerful incentive to sell shares of financial intermediaries, resulting in the destruction of approximately $200 billion in the market capitalization of the top twenty financial firms in the country during the two weeks running up to the failure of Bear Stearns. Given the predictable equity market reaction, public jawboning was not an effective means of strengthening bank capital structures.

The same unfortunate drama also played out over the spring and summer of 2008 with respect to the housing GSEs as Treasury and Federal Reserve officials urged the GSEs to raise new capital and equity markets drove their market capitalization lower.

Shift assets to the government's balance sheet. If the financial system, which contains the collective savings of households and business, cannot de-lever itself without a continued, precipitous decline of asset values, then the next logical response was to move assets to the government's balance sheet. The Bear Stearns and AIG facilities, provided by the Federal Reserve Bank of New York, have effectively transferred risk assets to the Federal Reserve's balance sheet and, indirectly via the Federal Reserve's income statement, to the Treasury. The Treasury's proposal for Congressional action that became the Troubled-Asset Relief Program (TARP) represented the major step in this direction and one that was also sound in concept but poorly executed.

The Treasury sensibly attempted to avoid the threat of dilution by underplaying the equity injection component. But the failure to effect asset transfers, which had been billed as the

TARP's principal purpose, contributed to a loss of the authorities' credibility and of public confidence. It is still hard to say whether the benefit of the additional capital injected into major firms was sufficient to offset the effects of the chaotic loss of confidence and the increase in uncertainty. The Federal Reserve's Commercial Paper Funding Facility (CPFF) is an example of another program intended to shift risks off of private sector balance sheets that was more effectively implemented.

Un-sterilized asset price support. As the Federal Reserve has continued to add to its numerous programs, their purpose appears to have shifted or, perhaps, become multi-faceted. Instead of simply absorbing risks from private balance sheets onto the public balance sheet through non-recourse lending, the Fed's actions now seem designed to influence or support the level of asset prices and to do so with an open-ended use of the Federal Reserve's ability to create money.

The Term Asset-Backed Securities Loan Facility (TALF) was designed to restore the securitization market by providing Fed financing for the purchase of securities, such as those backed by auto loans or credit card loans, as a means of ensuring the continued flow of credit. But what was first intended to support the flow of credit while the securitization market is disrupted has become a means of supporting the prices of securities, particularly now in conjunction with the Treasury's Public-Private Investment Program (PPIP), which aims to stimulate sufficient bids from investors to induce banks to sell their existing securities holdings to raise capital and reduce their balance sheets.

Finally, the outright purchases of Treasury securities, agency debt, and agency-backed mortgage-based securities by the Federal Reserve have been clearly intended to achieve a price effect so as to lower the cost and improve the availability of credit for households and businesses as part the Fed's "credit easing" policy.

What will be the consequences of the Federal Reserve's extraordinary balance sheet policies?

To explain the Federal Reserve's policies, Chairman Bernanke has used the analogy that if your neighbor's house is on fire because of his own bad habit of smoking in bed, you will still put the fire out first and worry about incentive effects later (see Bernanke 2009a). Given the risks of a self-reinforcing, downward spiral of falling asset values, confidence, and consumption leading to further declines in income and asset values, one should have some sympathy with the "put the fire out first" approach to public policy.

But exactly which fire is the Fed trying to put out? Why does the Fed think its actions can put out these particular flames? How does the Fed know that its balance sheet will act as water rather than oxygen?

Which fire? If the Fed is going to use its power to issue fiat currency in an experimental manner, it should meet an even-higher standard of transparency. We cannot reasonably expect the Fed to choose a point on the spectrum between rules and discretion, because the Fed is operating without a sufficient base of experience to have developed rules. But the Fed should conduct itself in a manner consistent with disciplined experimentation: the Fed can clearly state the objectives of each program, articulate a theory of how particular actions are intended to achieve the specific objective, and ensure the availability of data that they and we can use to measure the consistency or variance both of actions with theory and of outcomes with objectives.

The Fed's early policy actions to liberalize its lending facilities were articulated as serving the objective of bringing down short-term intra-bank lending spreads. These various programs rested on the theory that the provision of central bank collateralized liquidity would remove an uncertainty premium in unsecured intra-bank lending and a gradual narrowing of the short-term spreads has been observed.

This reduction in spreads may not have reflected the removal of an uncertainty or liquidity premium, or an improvement in the health of banks but, rather, only a substitution of massive central bank liquidity for intra-bank lending, effectively replacing an intra-bank market with central bank lifelines. But the Fed's clarity of purpose helped the market understand what the Fed was aiming to accomplish and helped establish the idea that an eventual decline in the use of these facilities would be a measure of success.

It has been harder to discern the specific objectives, theories, and measureable outcomes of the Fed's more recent credit easing policies, a point acknowledged by Chairman Bernanke.[3]

The broad objectives are self-evident: to stimulate aggregate demand by easing credit conditions through a mix of lending and purchases of securities. But what are the intermediate objectives? What's the theory? Does the Fed believe that it can control long-term interest rates and credit spreads by the

---

3. In a speech in January 2009, Bernanke noted that: "The lack of a simple summary measure or policy target poses an important communications challenge" (see Bernanke 2009b).

brute force of its balance sheet? Real rates? The term premium?
A credit premium? A liquidity premium?

Central banks as Hercules. Can the Fed, through purchases of
Treasury securities, compress the term premium to a level other
than that which reflects the expected path of monetary policy?
My prior assumption would have been not in an enduring way
or by more than a margin which reflects market participants' uncertainty about the expected path of monetary policy. The immediate impact of the announcement of the Fed's intent to
restart its purchases of Treasury securities appears to have lowered the yield on the 10-year Treasury by approximately half a
percent. Was this an enduring change in the term premium? It
is hard to say.

While open market purchases of Treasury securities might
push down on real rates in the short run, the extraordinary expansion of the Fed's liabilities is likely to be putting upward
pressure on the uncertainty premium and, thus, real rates.
Moreover, the purpose of the Fed's extraordinary actions is to
stimulate aggregate demand so as to return the economy more
promptly to full resource utilization and inflation rates of 2 percent or more. All of this should push up on the expected path
of monetary policy and, thus, on the term premium. So the Fed
appears to be both pushing down and pushing up on the term
structure at the same time. What's the optimal level? Does the
Fed have a view on the level of real rates that reflects a trade-
off between those "low" enough to stimulate aggregate demand
and those "high" enough to continue to attract foreign capital to finance our deficits?

Fed asset purchases could address a liquidity premium that
exists because of the paucity of buyers resulting from both the
"fire sale" of distressed sellers and the lack of dealer capital

to act as market makers. The Treasury's white paper which describes the PPIP makes just such a case (see Treasury Department 2009).

But market participants' balance sheets are fungible. As they sell inventory to the Fed, there is no guarantee that they will use their freed-up balance sheets for more of the assets whose prices the Fed seeks to influence or even that they will use that balance sheet capacity at all. While mortgage rates came down sharply immediately following the Fed's announcement in November of its intent to purchase agency mortgage-based securities, despite a significant increase in the level of Fed activity, and changes in many other factors since then, there has been little net change in mortgage rates since late November.

It is also hard to see how Fed purchases, or their equivalent in non-recourse lending, can compress credit premiums. While potential future losses can be shifted to the Fed's balance sheet through non-recourse lending, if there are one hundred units of credit in the market with a probability of default of x, and the Fed either buys or makes a non-recourse loan for half of them, the probability of default on the remaining fifty units in the market is still x.

Where's the exit? The Fed faces several "exit" problems. Most attention has focused on the eventual need for the Fed to withdraw the very high level of reserves caused by the expansion of the liability side of its balance sheet. While the Fed's technical ability to drain reserves when the time comes may be sufficient, or may need to be supplemented by new authority from Congress to issue longer-term liabilities, the Fed also faces a two-fold exit challenge on the asset side of its balance sheet.

Having undertaken "price-keeping operations" to compress

Treasury, mortgage, and other credit yields to affect an easing of financial conditions, the Fed will face the challenge of when and how to stop supporting asset prices. In the absence of a widely understood objective—other than asset price levels themselves—that market participants can independently assess, markets could become more volatile as participants anticipate the Fed ceasing its asset price support programs which, in turn, may cause the Fed to continue or prolong these operations.

While we know that the Fed's ultimate policy objectives are maximum sustainable employment consistent with price stability, what are its intermediate objectives for restoring the health of the financial system, independent of the level of asset prices themselves? What precisely does the Fed think of as the unusual and exigent circumstances that justify the use of Section 13(3) of the Federal Reserve Act? By what criteria will it decide when to stop?

In the Great Depression, instead of waiting to clean out the pipes of the old banking system that had become blocked, Congress created the Federal Home Loan Banks and effectively rebuilt our system of housing finance by erecting a new set of pipes which created the savings and loan industry as we knew it until the 1980s. After the S&L crisis of the 1980s, by lifting the constraints on the GSEs' balance sheets in the early 1990s instead of cleaning out the old system, we again effectively created a new structure for converting savings into investment, stimulated by the GSEs, which ran through the securitization markets. Today, the Fed is running the new set of pipes right through its own balance sheet. This puts the Fed in the odd position of competing with the banks whose cost of funds the Fed controls at the same time that it is trying to manage the level of asset prices—creating an even more complex set of incentive effects for credit market participants and the Federal Reserve to work out in the future.

REFERENCES

Bernanke, Ben S. (2008), "Reducing Preventable Mortgage Foreclosures," speech at the Independent Community Bankers of America Annual Convention, Orlando, FL, Mar. 4, available at www.federalreserve.gov/newsevents/speech/bernanke20080304a.htm.

Bernanke, Ben S. (2009a), interview remarks in the CBS program *60 Minutes*, Mar. 15, available at http://www.cbsnews.com/stories/2009/03/12/60minutes/main4862191.shtml.

Bernanke, Ben S. (2009b), "The Crisis and the Policy Response," remarks for the Stamp Lecture, London School of Economics, London, England, Jan. 13, available at www.federalreserve.gov/newsevents/speech/bernanke20090113a.htm.

Geithner, Timothy (2008), "The Current Financial Challenges: Policy and Regulatory Implications," speech at the Council on Foreign Relations Corporate Conference 2008, New York, NY, Mar. 6, available at www.newyorkfed.org/newsevents/speeches/2008/gei080306.html.

Treasury Department (2009), "Public-Private Investment Program," white paper, Mar. 23, available at www.treasury.gov/press/releases/reports/ppip_whitepaper_032309.pdf.

Part II:
The Fed's Entry and Exit Strategies

4

MONETARY POLICY IN THE FINANCIAL CRISIS

Donald L. Kohn

IN RESPONSE TO THE FINANCIAL TURMOIL and economic weakness of the past eighteen months, the Federal Reserve has taken unprecedented steps in conducting monetary policy. Not only have we reduced our target federal funds rate aggressively, essentially to zero, but we have also made credit available to institutions and markets in which we had not previously intervened. To varying degrees, similar actions have been taken by other central banks around the world.

Although our actions have been unprecedented, the framework in which I have been considering them remains, at its

These remarks were given at a conference honoring Dewey Daane on April 18, 2009, at Vanderbilt University. They are based on the comments I made at the workshop on the Future of Central Banking at the Hoover Institution on March 30, 2009. For other expositions of our monetary policy actions in the crisis, see Bernanke 2009a and Bernanke 2009b. The views presented here are my own and not necessarily those of other members of the Board of Governors or the Federal Open Market Committee.

most fundamental level, the same as the one I have been using as a policymaker over the years. Our objective is to promote maximum sustainable employment and stable prices over time. These goals are enshrined in law, and they also make sense in economic theory and practice. Central banks are uniquely suited to promoting price stability, and they contribute to maximum employment and growth over time by eliminating the uncertainties and distortions of high and unstable inflation. The goal of maximum employment also is critical: A balance between aggregate demand and potential supply is needed to maintain price stability; in addition, significant fluctuations in output impose costs on our economy, add to uncertainty, and impede planning and growth. Our monetary policy actions in the crisis have been aimed at fostering both broad objectives.[1]

We achieve our objectives by influencing financial conditions—the cost and availability of credit as well as asset prices. Changes in financial conditions, in turn, affect spending and thus the balance between aggregate demand and potential supply. And how close we are to maximum employment is a basic ongoing determinant of inflation, with slack reducing inflation and overly high resource utilization increasing it. The other major determinant is inflation expectations: If expectations are not anchored—if they vary in response to our actions or to persistent gaps between actual and potential output—inflation itself will follow.

---

1. My remarks will concentrate on actions aimed at broad sectors of the financial markets, not on those aimed at stabilizing individual systemically important institutions, like The Bear Stearns Companies, Inc.; American International Group, Inc., or AIG; and several bank holding companies.

Historically, we've achieved needed adjustments in financial conditions by moving our federal funds rate target, and we have done that by adjusting the supply of bank reserves through open market operations in the government securities market. In well-functioning financial markets, changes in actual and expected targets for the federal funds rate are arbitraged through the financial system to affect the cost of credit and the price of assets. Many factors affect these markets, and the relationship of our actions to financial conditions is very loose, but, on balance, we have been able to use our control of the federal funds rate to make the adjustments to financial conditions needed to foster our objectives for prices and employment.

From the time that the financial market turmoil emerged in force in August 2007, however, we could see that the relationship of the federal funds rate to financial conditions, and hence to spending, was especially disrupted, with any given federal funds rate implying much tighter conditions than usual. Banks became quite uncertain about the losses they might have to absorb on mortgages and other lending, about the losses their counterparties might also suffer, and about the extent to which their liquidity was at risk from having to support off-balance-sheet entities or from experiencing a withdrawal by their own lenders. This uncertainty made banks much more cautious about extending credit to each other and to households and businesses. As financial disruption continued and the economy weakened, lenders generally became much more uncertain about the financial condition of borrowers, sparking a strong preference for safe and liquid assets like Treasury bills. Trading liquidity in many markets dried up, the usual arbitrage among markets broke down, and spreads widened—often by more than seemed justified by the underlying deterioration in the economy and the ability of borrowers to repay. The tightening of financial conditions, in turn, further restrained aggregate demand and economic activity. This adverse feedback loop between financial conditions and the economy has been a prominent feature of the recession.

The Federal Reserve took a two-pronged approach to countering the effects of financial stringency on the economy: We used our conventional policy tools, and we initiated a range of unconventional policy actions to support the extension of credit. In the first category, we cut the federal funds rate target and did so aggressively after the economy began to weaken substantially in late 2007. By December of last year, we had reduced the target to a range of 0 to 1/4 percent. Lowering the federal funds rate helped offset a portion of the effects of financial disruption on credit conditions for households and businesses. And policy easing should have helped the flow of credit by reducing some of the concerns about the effects of a weaker economy on repayment prospects.

But reducing the federal funds rate has not seemed sufficient, and so we also have taken actions to ease conditions in credit markets more directly—what Chairman Bernanke has referred to as "credit easing." In many respects, these actions have been extensions of our traditional methods of operation, though they have taken us into new territory in which we have used the tools in very new ways.

Beginning early in the turmoil, we eased the terms on which we lent to depository institutions (our traditional borrowers) quite dramatically. We lowered the interest rate on discount window loans, increased their maturity, and, to reduce the stigma of borrowing from the window, auctioned credit. We cooperated with foreign central banks through currency swaps to make dollar funding available to banks operating abroad. Later, for the first time since the 1930s, we extended credit to nondepository institutions, granting discount window access to primary dealers when it became evident that constraints on their access to liquidity threatened broader financial stability and economic activity.[2] Given the increasing reliance on securities markets to intermediate credit in our financial system, these dealers had become more central to maintaining the flow of credit from savers to borrowers. Last fall, when a run on money market mutual funds was severely constricting their purchases of commercial paper, an important source of credit to many businesses, we supported the funds, their customers, and their borrowers by making credit available that allowed funds to meet heavy redemption requests and also provided credit directly to borrowers in the commercial paper market.

Our objectives in these programs are consistent with central banks' classic function as lenders of last resort. We are encouraging the continued provision of private-sector funding to intermediaries by assuring their creditors that sound intermediaries have a sure source of liquidity to repay debts. When, despite this encouragement, private lenders have such a strong preference for safety and liquidity that credit is not forthcoming, we lend, often at a penalty rate relative to normally functioning markets; that lending is intended to prevent disorderly and disruptive failures and fire sales of illiquid assets, which would drive asset prices lower, intensify the disruption of credit flows, and deepen the pullback in spending.

---

2. Primary dealers are broker-dealers that trade in U.S. government securities with the Federal Reserve Bank of New York.

Most recently, in collaboration with the Treasury, we have begun supplying liquidity to purchasers of securitized credit. Under this program, private investors absorb credit risk up to a certain level, and the Treasury takes on the bulk of the credit risk above that level. The Federal Reserve's residual credit risk is designed to be quite small. The asset-backed securities market that this program is designed to support had become a key vehicle over the past couple of decades for financing credit extended to households and businesses, but its functioning deteriorated rapidly over the second half of last year, with issuance tailing off almost completely. The availability of credit from the Federal Reserve and the insurance against severe downside risks from the Treasury should buoy demand for securitized debt and thus help bolster the flow of credit to households and businesses.

A shortage of funding has not been the only factor impeding the extension of credit. Lenders have been concerned about counterparty risk and about conserving their own capital against unforeseeable events. We can't deal with those concerns through our lending because we do not take appreciable credit risk. But confidence about access to funding has been a part of the problem, as reflected in the evaporation of trading in term maturities in a wide range of wholesale funding markets and the elevated spreads paid by even very safe borrowers. The limited availability of credit to sound borrowers, even when secured by what had been seen as good collateral, has been a source of instability and constraint on credit flows. Central banks can address such a shortage because they can remain unaffected by panicky flights to liquidity and safety. Their willingness to extend collateralized lending in size against a broad range of assets can replace flows of private credit that are normally uncollateralized.

Another aspect of our efforts to affect financial conditions has been the extension of our open market operations to large-scale purchases of agency mortgage-backed securities (MBS), agency debt, and longer-term Treasury debt. We initially announced our intention to undertake large-scale asset purchases last November, when the federal funds rate began to approach its zero lower bound and we needed to begin applying stimulus through other channels as the economic contraction deepened. These purchases are intended to reduce intermediate- and longer-term interest rates on mortgages and other credit to households and businesses; those rates influence decisions about investments in long-lived assets like houses, consumer durable goods, and business capital. In ordinary circumstances, the typically quite modest volume of central bank purchases and sales of such assets has only small and temporary effects on their yields. However, the extremely large volume of purchases now underway does appear to have substantially lowered yields. The decline in yields reflects "preferred habitat" behavior, meaning that there is not perfect arbitrage between the yields on longer-term assets and current and expected short-term interest rates. These preferences are likely to be especially strong in current circumstances, so that long-term asset prices rise and yields fall as the Federal Reserve acquires a significant portion of the outstanding stock of securities held by the public.

Against this general background, let me address some questions about our operations.

HAVE THEY BEEN EFFECTIVE?

Yes, I believe they have helped ease financial conditions, though they can't address all the problems in financial markets. And the situation in financial markets and the economy would have been far worse if the Federal Reserve hadn't taken the actions we did in supplying liquidity as well as lowering our federal funds rate target.

Clearly, sharp decreases in the federal funds rate target have shown up directly in other short-term interest rates. Our commercial paper facilities helped stabilize money market mutual funds and have steadied the commercial paper market and lowered rates for high-quality issuers. And the announcements of our purchases of MBS and Treasury bonds have reduced mortgage and other long-term interest rates appreciably—by some estimates as many as 100 basis points.

Our provision of liquidity to banks in the United States and, via currency swaps with other central banks, abroad appears to have eased pressures in dollar funding markets, as indicated by declines in spreads between the London interbank offered rate (Libor) and the overnight index swap rate. This easing has lowered rates for bank borrowers paying rates tied to Libor and given banks better access to interbank liquidity to support lending and market making. The extension of liquidity to primary dealers has been critical in providing stability when private lenders have, from time to time, become reluctant to make even secured loans to these counterparties. Our own sense, reinforced by many reports from market participants, is that our willingness to extend credit to commercial and investment banks prevented far worse market outcomes when flights to liquidity and safety intensified—say, around the time of the problems of Bear Stearns and in the wake of multiple failures and near-failures of financial firms in the second half of September. Private lenders have demanded that intermediaries be much less leveraged. That development is healthy over the long run, but when the transition is compressed by extreme risk aversion and market participants are forced to delever through fire sales, the financial markets and economy suffer. Our liquidity facilities allow for a more gradual and controlled process.

Are We Allocating Credit?

Our actions are aimed at increasing credit flows for the entire economy; we are not trying to favor some sectors over others. However, an element of credit allocation is inherent in some of our interventions. That element grows out of the very market characteristics that have necessitated these interventions and have made such interventions effective. If markets were highly liquid and investors and lenders were willing to take normal risks and arbitrage across markets, financial conditions wouldn't have tightened so much, intensifying the economic downturn, and adjustments in the federal funds rate could well have sufficed to stabilize the economy. As we have been forced to attack overly tight financial conditions by extending our discount window facilities to new intermediaries and certain markets and to extend open market operations to agency debt and MBS, we have recognized that the resulting effects can be uneven across markets and lenders. This outcome is not a comfortable one for the central bank, and we have taken steps to minimize the extent of any credit allocation. We try to limit our interventions to broad market segments or classes of intermediaries, and we choose them based on judgments that improved functioning will reduce systemic instability or have a material effect on credit flows and the economy and that our actions have high odds of yielding improvements.

ARE WE TAKING CREDIT RISKS THAT WILL END UP BEING PAID FOR BY THE TAXPAYER?

For the credit facilities that we make available to multiple firms, we are not taking significant credit risk that might end up being absorbed by the taxpayer. For almost all the loans made by the Federal Reserve, we look first to sound borrowers for repayment and then to underlying collateral. Moreover, we lend less than the value of the collateral, with the size of the "haircuts" depending on the riskiness of the collateral and on the availability of market prices for the collateral. Some of our lending programs involve nonrecourse loans that look primarily to the collateral rather than to the borrower for repayment in the event that the value of the collateral falls below the amount loaned. In these circumstances, we insist on taking only the very highest quality collateral, lend less than the face amount of the collateral, and typically have other sources to absorb any losses that might nonetheless occur—for example, Treasury capital for our lending against securitized loans.[3]

We have increased the amount of information that we publish about the collateral and other steps we take to protect

---

3. Loans or credit protection offered in association with government help to stabilize individual systemically important institutions probably have higher credit risk than the more general liquidity facilities described in this talk. But even in those cases, the Federal Reserve has taken steps to protect itself from credit losses.

against credit losses. But, understandably, given the sharp increase in loans to new institutions and markets, the public is naturally interested in our lending practices, and we will be releasing even more information about what stands behind our loans in coming weeks.

How Will We Gauge How Much to Do?

This is a difficult question without a ready answer, even under more normal circumstances when we are focused on the federal funds rate, and it is an even harder judgment when, as now, the federal funds rate is near zero and we are intervening in other ways to affect financial conditions. We have some, albeit limited, ability to gauge the effects of large-scale asset purchases on interest rates; the effects of liquidity facilities, like the Term Asset-Backed Securities Loan Facility and other programs, are even more difficult to assess and predict. And with markets disrupted and confidence depressed, the relationship between a particular constellation of interest rates and asset prices and future spending and inflation is more uncertain than usual. We will continue to analyze these relationships in light of our experience and adjust our forecast of the evolution of the economy under various policy alternatives, but we need to recognize that those forecasts could change appreciably and be ready to adapt policy flexibly. That flexibility could entail doing more to ease credit if the economy proves resistant to the monetary and fiscal stimulus now in train, or it could involve reversing actions to forestall potential inflationary effects of past actions, as I will discuss in a moment.

In gauging the effects of market interventions in the current crisis, one approach is to look to the size of increases in the quantity of reserves and money to judge whether sufficient liquidity is being provided to forestall deflation and support a turnaround in growth—an approach often known as quantitative easing. The linkages between reserves and money and between either reserves or money and nominal spending are highly variable and not especially reliable under normal circumstances. And the relationships among these variables become even more tenuous when so many short-term interest rates are pinned near zero and monetary and some nonmonetary assets are near-perfect substitutes. In our approach to policy, the amount of reserves has been a result of our market interventions rather than a goal in itself. And, depending on the circumstances, declines in reserves may indicate that markets are improving, not that policy is effectively tightening or failing to lean against weaker demand. Still, we on the Federal Open Market Committee (FOMC) recognize that high levels of Federal Reserve assets and resulting reserves are likely to be essential to fostering recovery, and we have discussed whether some explicit objectives for growth in the size of our balance sheet or for the quantity of the monetary base or reserves would provide some assurance that policy is pointed in the right direction.

WILL THESE POLICIES LEAD TO A FUTURE SURGE IN INFLATION?

No, and the key to preventing inflation will be reversing the programs, reducing reserves, and raising interest rates in a timely fashion. Our balance sheet has grown rapidly, the amount of reserves has skyrocketed, and announced plans imply further huge increases in Federal Reserve assets and bank reserves. Nonetheless, the size of our balance sheet will not preclude our raising interest rates when that becomes appropriate for macroeconomic stability. Many of the liquidity programs are authorized only while circumstances in the economy and financial markets are "unusual and exigent," and such programs will be terminated when conditions are no longer so adverse. Those programs and others have been designed to be unattractive in normal market conditions and will naturally wind down as markets improve.

However, our newly purchased Treasury securities and MBS will not mature or be repaid for many years; the loans we are making to back the securitization market are for three years, and their nonrecourse feature could leave us with assets thereafter. But we have a number of tools we can use to absorb the resulting reserves and raise interest rates when the time comes. We can sell the Treasury and agency debt either on an outright basis or temporarily through reverse repurchase agreements, and we are developing the capability to do the same with MBS. We are paying interest on excess reserves, which we can use to help provide a floor for the federal funds rate, as it does for other central banks, even if declines in lending or open market operations are not sufficient to bring reserves down to the desired level. Finally, we are working with the Treasury to promote legislation that would further enhance our toolkit for absorbing reserves.

Our work on the framework for exiting these programs is one indication that we are focused on maintaining price stability over time even as we concentrate for now on promoting economic recovery. Another such indication is our increased emphasis on defining the price stability goal more clearly. Already the FOMC has extended its forecast horizon to indicate where the Governors and Reserve Bank presidents would like to see inflation coming to rest over time. And we are continuing to discuss within the Committee whether an explicit numerical objective for inflation would be beneficial. Under current circumstances, those benefits would include underscoring our understanding that our legislative mandate for promoting price stability encompasses both preventing inflation from falling too low in the near term and from rising too far as the economy recovers.

HAVE WE COMPROMISED OUR INDEPENDENCE?

No. Central banks all over the world and the legislatures that created them have recognized that considerable independence from short-run political influences is essential for the conduct of monetary policy that promotes economic growth and price stability. To be sure, in the process of combating financial instability, we have needed to cooperate in unprecedented ways with the Treasury. Our actions with the Treasury to support individual systemically important institutions have sparked intense public and legislative interest. As Chairman Bernanke has indicated, the absence of a regime for resolving systemically important nonbank financial institutions has been a serious deficiency in the current crisis, one that the Congress needs to remedy. Congress and the public, quite appropriately, want to know more about lending programs that have greatly increased the scope and size of the Federal Reserve's interventions in financial markets, and we will give them that information. In addition, our country, like others, is undertaking a broad examination of what changes are needed in our financial regulatory system. This examination will consider the role of the Federal Reserve in the supervision and regulation of financial institutions and the advantages and disadvantages of establishing a systemic risk authority.

It is natural and appropriate for our unusual actions in combating financial instability and recession to come under intense scrutiny. However, increased attention to, and occasional criticism of, our activities should not lead to a fundamental change in our place within our democracy. And I believe it will not; the essential role for an independent monetary policy authority pursuing economic growth and price stability remains widely appreciated and the Federal Reserve has played that role well over the years. The recent joint statement of the Treasury and the Federal Reserve included an agreement to pursue further tools to control our balance sheet, indicating the Administration's recognition of the importance of our ability to independently pursue our macroeconomic objectives (see Board of Governors 2009).

Conclusion

The Federal Reserve's actions over the past twenty months have been consistent with the principles of central banking that have been developed over the course of centuries. But the greatly increased complexity of our financial institutions and markets, as well as the virulence of the financial crisis in choking off the flow of credit through a broad range of channels, has meant that in applying these principles, the Federal Reserve and other central banks have had to extend their reach and adopt new measures to preserve financial stability and to counter the effects of financial turmoil on the economy. In my view, these actions have been necessary, safe, and effective and will not lead to adverse aftereffects. But they have raised a number of questions that I have addressed today. These questions are very much in the forefront of our considerations as we formulate and implement policies to combat the severe disruptions to the financial markets and the economy, and we are determined that the answers to them remain consistent with both recovery from recession and the longer-run economic welfare of our Nation.

References

Bernanke, Ben S. (2009a), "The Federal Reserve's Balance Sheet," speech delivered at the Federal Reserve Bank of Richmond 2009 Credit Markets Symposium, Charlotte, N.C., April 3, 2009, available at www.federalreserve.gov/newsevents/speech/bernanke20090403a.htm.

Bernanke, Ben S. (2009b), "The Crisis and the Policy Response," speech delivered at the Stamp Lecture, London School of Economics, London, January 13, 2009, available at www.federalreserve.gov/newsevents/speech/bernanke20090113a.htm.

Board of Governors of the Federal Reserve System and U.S. Department of the Treasury (2009), "The Role of the Federal Reserve in Preserving Financial and Monetary Stability: Joint Statement by the Department of the Treasury and the Federal Reserve," joint press release, March 23, 2009, available at www.federalreserve.gov/newsevents/press/monetary/20090323b.htm.

5

CONCERNS ABOUT THE FED'S NEW BALANCE SHEET

James D. Hamilton

THE TRADITIONAL TOOL of monetary policy is an open market operation, in which the Federal Reserve purchases short-term Treasury securities from the public. The Fed pays for these purchases by crediting the deposits that the selling bank holds in an account with the Fed. These deposits can be thought of as electronic credits for cash, which banks could withdraw in the form of green currency whenever banks wished. The primary goal of open market operations was understood to be to control the available supply of reserve deposits and the money supply in order to achieve policy targets for the short-term interest rate and inflation.

If the Fed wanted to increase the supply of reserve deposits on a strictly temporary basis, it would traditionally do so with a repurchase agreement (repo), acquiring an asset from the counterparty and crediting the counterparty's Fed balance with newly created deposits, with an explicit agreement to return the asset and receive the deposits plus interest back at a specified future date. Essentially repos represent a collateral-ized short-term loan from the Fed to private banks, which had traditionally been the Fed's favored method for effecting a temporary increase in reserve deposits.

Figure 1 displays the assets held by the Federal Reserve each week between January 2003 and June 2007. Treasury securities represented by far the most important asset over this period. The volume of repurchase agreements was much smaller than Treasuries held outright, and the high week-to-week volatility of repos resulted from the way in which this tool was used to

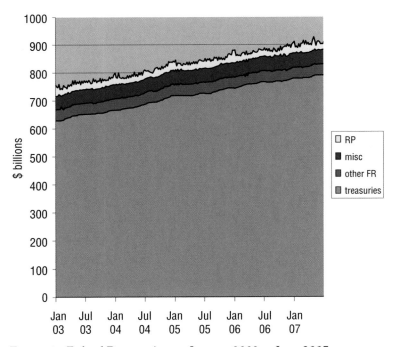

FIGURE 1. **Federal Reserve Assets, January 2003 to June 2007**

NOTES: Wednesday values, seasonally unadjusted, from Federal Reserve H41 release. Definitions of these and other legend entries are included at the end of this chapter.

meet strictly temporary liquidity needs over this period. Other assets held by the Fed usually changed little from week to week.

Figure 2 shows the liabilities of the Federal Reserve over this same period. By definition, the value of all the assets in Figure 1 at any given date is exactly equal to value of all the liabilities shown in Figure 2. Federal Reserve deposits represent the sum of the components labeled "service" and "reserves" in Figure 2. One sees from the figure that the reserve deposits that were created as a result of open market purchases over this period soon ended up as currency held by the public. One can think of monetary policy over this period essentially as a

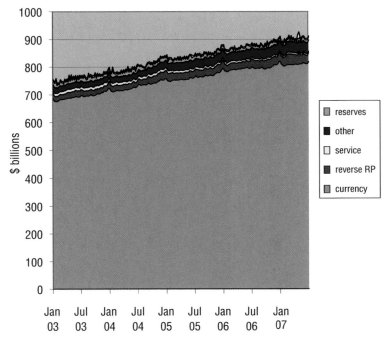

FIGURE 2. **Federal Reserve Liabilities, January 2003 to June 2007**
NOTES: Wednesday values, seasonally unadjusted, from Federal Reserve H41 release.

process of exchanging currency created by the Fed for T-bills held by the public.

In August of 2007, strains on several European banks resulted in a sharp spike in interbank lending rates that proved to be the beginning of a new era of credit concerns. As seen in Figure 3, the Fed began to explore alternative policy instruments to deal with these challenges. The first step was a permanent expansion in the volume of outstanding repo operations at any given date. By August 27, 2008, these had risen to $111 billion. The Fed was using these operations not for the traditional purpose of temporarily adding to the supply of reserve deposits, but instead was hoping for some benefits from the collateral side of the operation itself. By accepting otherwise illiquid securities as collateral for the repo, the Fed was hoping to narrow the spread between the yield on T-bills and the borrowing costs of the institutions holding the problematic assets. The Fed also began central bank liquidity swaps, lending dollars temporarily to foreign central banks, with $67 billion lent through these operations as of August 27, 2008. The biggest new operation over this period was the Term Auction Facility, which had loaned $150 billion to depository institutions as of the end of August.

Although the Fed described these operations as "providing liquidity," they were not doing so in the traditional sense of increasing the supply of available reserves. At the same time that the Fed was lending to banks through the Term Auction Facility (which would have created $150 billion in new reserves), it was simultaneously selling off its holdings of T-bills, with the deliberate intention of preventing these new operations from affecting the money supply, the fed funds rate, or inflation. The purpose of the Term Auction Facility was thus not to get

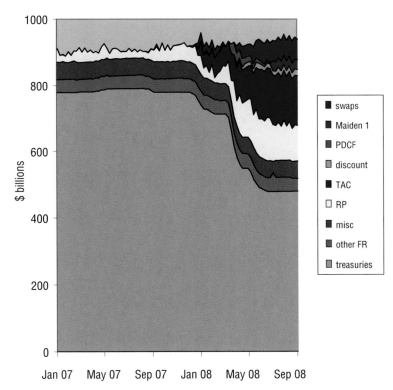

FIGURE 3. Federal Reserve Assets, January 2007 to August 2008

NOTES. Wednesday values, seasonally unadjusted, from Federal Reserve H41 release.

additional reserves into the banking system, but instead to support the value of the assets accepted as collateral and the institutions that held these assets. In terms of the liabilities side of the Fed balance sheet, little changed between January 2007 and August 2008 (see Figure 4).

The Fed's balance sheet entered a new phase of dramatic changes after the failure of Lehman Brothers in September 2008 and attendant freezing of many important credit markets.

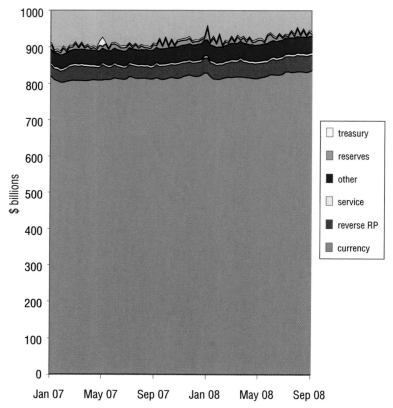

FIGURE 4. Federal Reserve Liabilities, January 2007 to August 2008

NOTES. Wednesday values, seasonally unadjusted, from Federal Reserve H41 release.

The Fed expanded Term Auction Credit to a value currently near half a trillion, and currency swaps to a third of a trillion, as well as initiating a host of new lending facilities, the biggest of which at the moment is a quarter trillion dollars of holdings of the Commercial Paper Lending Facility. The Fed also acquired $89 billion in assets related to maintaining the solvency of insurer AIG, and has recently purchased $236 billion in mortgage-backed securities. Altogether, these new facilities and operations have led to an expansion of Federal Reserve assets from $940 billion on September 3 to $2.1 trillion on March 25 (see Figure 5).

The Fed did not own enough Treasury securities to sterilize these operations as it had those through August of 2008 via offsetting sales of T-bills. Nevertheless, it was still the intention

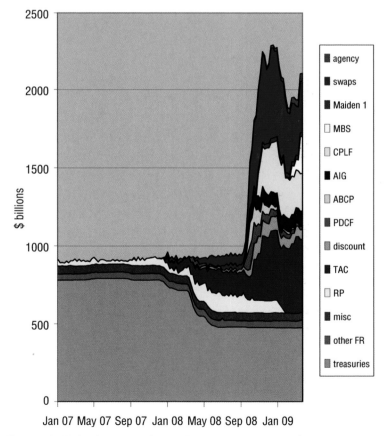

FIGURE 5. **Federal Reserve Assets, January 2007 to March 2008**

NOTES. Wednesday values, seasonally unadjusted, from Federal Reserve H41 release.

of the Fed that these operations should not affect the total currency in circulation. The Fed took two steps to prevent any consequences of the new facilities for the total quantity of currency in circulation. The first action was to request that the Treasury borrow some funds directly and simply leave the funds deposited in an account with the Fed. This operation by itself would have been equivalent to an open-market sale of Treasuries by the Fed. When the buyer of the T-bill delivers funds to the Treasury's account with the Fed, those reserves are drained back out of the private banking system. The reserves so drained by the Treasury accounts (which totaled $256 billion as of March 25) were in fact the same reserves created by some of the Fed's new facilities (see Figure 6).

To fund the rest of the expansion of the Fed's assets without impacting the volume of currency held by the public, the Fed adopted a policy of promising to pay the same interest rate on reserves as its target for the fed funds rate itself. In effect, this makes reserve deposits (now an interest-bearing liability of the Fed) similar to T-bills themselves (an interest-bearing liability of the Treasury), and potentially eliminates the need to get the Treasury involved in raising the funds needed for the assorted new Fed facilities. Given that lending reserves to another bank on the fed funds market involves some risk, whereas simply holding them as deposits with the Fed does not, paying interest on reserves greatly increases the demand for reserves. Indeed, most of the new reserve deposits created by the Fed ended up simply being held as excess reserves, the magnitude of which was $818 billion as of March 25. As a result of the Treasury borrowing and ballooning excess reserves, the more than doubling in the size of the Fed's balance sheet has so far had limited effect on the total currency in circulation.

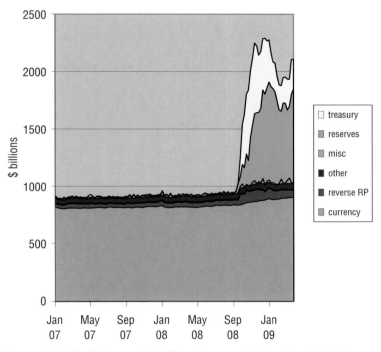

FIGURE 6. **Federal Reserve Liabilities, January 2007 to March 2008**

NOTES. Wednesday values, seasonally unadjusted, from Federal Reserve H41 release.

The new Fed balance sheet represents a profound change in the basic mission of monetary policy. In the traditional open market operation, the Fed does not become involved in the decision of where credit gets allocated. It simply creates the quantity of reserves that it deems most desirable for aggregate economic performance, and lets the market sort out which banks actually end up holding those reserves. By injecting these reserves through the practice of paying the market price for a highly liquid previously issued T-bill, the Fed traditionally was neither allocating newly created wealth to any particular party nor directing it to any chosen function.

By contrast, the philosophy behind the new Fed balance sheet is very much to try to choose directly which markets receive the benefits from newly created reserves. That new philosophy raises in my mind three potential concerns.

My first worry is whether the Fed is indeed making the correct choices as to which segments of the capital market are most worthy of assistance. As a general principle, I would think that in a normally functioning capital market, such decisions are better made on the basis of investors deciding where their own funds could earn the highest private return rather than by intelligent and well-meaning government officials. Suppose we grant, for the sake of discussion, that capital markets are presently not so functioning, and that a large government role in making decisions as to where credit gets allocated is unavoidable in the present circumstance. There nevertheless remains the practical question of which lending is most beneficial from a social perspective at the current time.

On these narrow grounds alone, I have profound misgivings about the Term Asset-Backed Securities Loan Facility (TALF), which is currently under $5 billion, but was envisioned to grow to a $200 billion commitment from the Fed in support of a trillion dollars in asset-backed securities created from new auto loans, credit card loans, student loans, and SBA-guaranteed small business loans. A press release issued jointly by the Treasury Department and the Federal Reserve described the vision behind this proposal as follows:

> The TALF is designed to catalyze the securitization markets by providing financing to investors to support their purchases of certain AAA-rated asset-backed securities (ABS). These markets have historically been a critical component

of lending in our financial system, but they have been virtually shuttered since the worsening of the financial crisis in October. By reopening these markets, the TALF will assist lenders in meeting the borrowing needs of consumers and small businesses, helping to stimulate the broader economy. (See U.S. Treasury 2009.)

Securitization is a process whereby a group of separate loans gets pooled together. The income flow from the pool is divided among a set of newly created securities designated as separate "tranches," with the senior tranches receiving priority payment. The result is that the senior tranches are less risky than the original underlying loans, while the junior tranches are more risky. The theory was that the added safety provided by the senior tranches might bring investment capital into these markets that would otherwise be unavailable, while a higher expected return on the junior tranches could compensate the holders of these for the extra risk. There is no question that securitization had been a phenomenally successful device for attracting capital to private loan markets in recent years.

Ashcraft and Schuermann (2008) studied details of the securitization of a pool of about 4,000 subprime mortgage loans whose principal value came to a little under $900 million. These loans were originated by New Century Financial in the second quarter of 2006, a company that was to declare bankruptcy less than a year later. Most of these loans called for a huge increase in the monthly payments from households for which one would have significant questions as to their ability to make the current payments. Ashcraft and Schuermann found that 79% of the notional value of securities created were rated Aaa by both Standard and Poor's and Moody's, with only 5% of the notional value receiving less than an A- from S&P or A3 from Moody's. To put those ratings in perspective, only five U.S. companies are currently in a position to issue Aaa-rated debt.

Those high ratings were unquestionably successful in attracting a huge flow of capital into these lending markets, facilitating the origination of $4.3 trillion in new non-agency mortgage loans between 2004 and 2006. U.S. household mortgage debt tripled in a little over a decade.

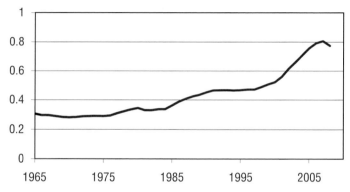

FIGURE 7. Ratio of Home Mortgage Debt to GDP, 1965–2008

NOTES. Home mortgage debt (from Federal Reserve Board Flow of Funds, Table L.2), divided by nominal GDP (annual figures).

I would be greatly troubled if members of the FOMC were unprepared to acknowledge that those capital flows during 2004–2006 represented a profound mistake. We surely can all see now that the high ratings associated with much of the securitized debt were completely inappropriate. Investors bought this debt because they were fundamentally mistaken in believing that securitization could somehow provide safety from aggregate risk factors common to the loans in the pool. Rather than a device that improved the functioning of asset markets, at least over the period 2003–2006, securitization succeeded primarily because it misled investors into thinking that certain investments were safer than in actuality they were. The whole premise that there are vast sources of capital that are uninterested in funding an institution that simply buys and holds the pool of loans in its entirety, but nevertheless have huge demands for each of its tailored tranches, seems to me highly dubious. That the Fed would choose to try to return us to such a system strikes me as a refusal to acknowledge that capital markets were previously profoundly misallocating resources in a way that was unsustainable and indeed was the primary cause of our present difficulties.

A second concern I have about the Fed's new balance sheet is that I believe it has seriously compromised the independence of the central bank. The decision of where public funds are best allocated is inherently political. Any risks on the Fed's new balance sheet are ultimately borne by the taxpayers. The U.S. Constitution specifies that decisions of how public funds get spent shall be up to Congress, and with good reason. Citizens have a right to vote on which risks they choose to absorb. And of course there are powerful established interests with views on which sectors should receive an infusion of public capital. The Fed is simply being naive if it thinks it can become involved in those decisions on a weekly basis and yet still retain its independence from Congress and the President.

The reason I find that loss of Fed independence to be a source of alarm is the observation that every hyperinflation in history has had two ingredients. The first is a fiscal debt for which there was no politically feasible ability to pay with tax increases or spending cuts. The second is a central bank that was drawn into the task of creating money as the only way to meet the obligations that the fiscal authority could not. Every historical hyperinflation has ended when the fiscal problems got resolved and independence of the central bank was restored.

Surely it is not far-fetched to suggest that the U.S. faces a profound political challenge in using spending cuts or tax increases to meet its current and planned fiscal obligations. Here's an observation that brought that reality home to me on a personal level: in fiscal year 2006, receipts collected by the U.S. federal government from personal income taxes totaled $1.06 trillion. Thus, to a first approximation of what an extra trillion dollars in taxes would mean for me personally, I just take the number I paid in 2006 and double it. And then I ask myself, how likely is it that Congress would actually do such a thing? With budget deficits in excess of a trillion dollars annually for the foreseeable future, it seems we are already well past the point at which the ability of the Treasury to fund the expanded liabilities through tax increases would reasonably be questioned.

Moreover, the detailed cooperation between the Fed and the Treasury in the various new credit measures seems to have arisen from precisely such pressures. Congress is, in fact, unwilling to accept explicitly the risks to which taxpayers are exposed as a result of the many new Fed-Treasury initiatives. If I were the chair of the Federal Reserve, I would want to be asking, "Why was I invited to this party?" The answer unfortunately appears to be "Because you're the one with the deep pockets." That the Fed should find itself in a position where

Congress and the White House are viewing its ability to print money as an asset to fund initiatives they otherwise couldn't afford is something that should give pause to any self-respecting central banker.

My third concern about the new Fed balance sheet is that it has seriously handicapped the Fed's ability to fulfill its primary mission of promoting price stability. We arrived at the current situation because the Fed was deliberately trying to insulate any consequences of its actions for the quantity of currency in circulation, first by selling T-bills at the same time it was expanding new facilities, and later by asking the Treasury to borrow on its behalf and taking steps to encourage the accumulation of excess reserves. However, in 2008:Q4 and 2009:Q1 we reached a point where there was an actual decrease in the general price level and concerns by many about the prospect of significant further deflation. I think we can all agree that deflation would be quite counterproductive to economic recovery. There are disturbing parallels between the current situation—low nominal interest rate but potentially high real interest rate—and the problems experienced by the United States in the 1930s or Japan in the 1990s.

In the current environment, we would be substantially better off with 2–3% inflation than with the realized deflation, and better off with a nominal 1% interest rate that, given those inflation rates, implied real stimulus. But precisely because of the changes in the Fed's balance sheet, this may be very difficult for the Fed to deliver. Among the challenges is the fact that, if the Fed does successfully convince the public that it will ensure a low level of inflation rather than deflation, it may prove impossible to contain fears of a substantial surge in inflation. To address those concerns, the Fed would need the ability to quickly absorb back in the dollars it creates, namely to quickly sell off the many new assets it's acquired. Yet the Fed's current portfolio would prove extremely difficult to liquidate on a short-term basis. And insofar as those inflation fears take the form of concerns about how the Treasury is going to roll over its burgeoning debt, the Fed would lack the resources to dispel such concerns.

We thus find ourselves in a situation where half the public fears we're about to experience a severe deflation, and the other half believes we're about to experience an unstoppable hyperinflation. While the powers of a central bank are fundamentally limited, the destabilizing consequences of such fears should be the one thing that the central bank unambiguously has the power to prevent. What we need above all else in the current situation is a Federal Reserve on which the world can count as a bulwark of stability, and the dollar itself as an asset of reliable value.

The Fed would be much better able to fulfill that role if its balance sheet looked like Figures 1 and 2 than if it looked like Figures 5 and 6.

To the extent that the Fed moves beyond traditional purchases of short-term Treasury bills—and I agree that is necessary in the current situation—it should be buying assets whose value, particularly in the face of a sudden surge in inflationary expectations, is unquestioned. Making outright purchases of longer term Treasury Inflation Protected Securities until we achieve the desired expansion of currency in circulation and overall prices would seem to me to be the ideal solution.

References

Ashcraft, Adam B. and Til Schuermann, "Understanding the securitization of subprime mortgage credit," working paper, Federal Reserve Bank of New York, 2008.

U.S. Treasury Department and Federal Reserve Board, "U.S. Treasury and Federal Reserve Board Announce Launch of Term Asset-Backed Securities Loan Facility (TALF)," March 3, 2009, posted at www.financialstability.gov/latest/tg45.html and by the Federal Reserve at www.federalreserve.gov/newsevents/press/monetary/20090303a.htm.

Legend Key for Figures

Fed Assets (Figures 1, 3, and 5)

ABCP—loans extended to Asset-Backed Commercial Paper Money Market Mutual Fund Liquidity Facility

Agency—federal agency debt securities held outright

AIG—sum of credit extended to American International Group, Inc. plus net portfolio holdings of Maiden Lane II and III

CPLF—net portfolio holdings of LLCs funded through the Commercial Paper Funding Facility

Discount—sum of primary credit, secondary credit, and seasonal credit

Maiden 1—net portfolio holdings of Maiden Lane LLC

MBS—mortgage-backed securities held outright

Misc—sum of float, gold stock, special drawing rights certificate account, and Treasury currency outstanding

Other FR—other Federal Reserve assets

PDCF—loans extended to primary dealer and other broker-dealer credit

RP—repurchase agreements

Swaps—central bank liquidity swaps

TAC—term auction credit

Treasuries—U.S. Treasury securities held outright

Fed Liabilities (Figures 2, 4, and 6)

Currency—currency in circulation

Misc—sum of Treasury cash holdings, foreign official accounts, and other deposits

Other—other liabilities and capital

Reserves—reserve balances with Federal Reserve Banks

Reverse RP—reverse repurchase agreements

Service—sum of required clearing balance and adjustments to compensate for float

Treasury—sum of U.S. Treasury general and supplementary funding accounts

6

THE NEED FOR A CLEAR AND CREDIBLE EXIT STRATEGY

John B. Taylor

THE FED IS NOW OPERATING a completely unprecedented policy regime. While there is disagreement about the appropriateness of the extraordinary measures that constitute this regime, few disagree that, at some time, the Fed should exit from it and return to traditional monetary policy: controlling money growth and adjusting the short-term interest rate to keep inflation low and the economy stable. In my view, the financial crisis was caused, prolonged, and worsened by the Fed's departure from traditional monetary policy—even if some of the recent actions have been useful as a means of cleaning up the damage (see Taylor 2009a). Hence, it is essential that the Fed develop and clarify a credible exit strategy from the current policy to the type of regime that delivered good economic performance for several decades. Here I discuss some principles that underlie such an exit strategy.

EXPLODING RESERVES

To understand the magnitude of the problem, first consider the extraordinary increase in reserve balances at the Fed, as shown in Figure 1. Reserve balances, or deposits at the Fed, are the key component—along with currency—of base money or central bank money, which the Federal Reserve is responsible for controlling and which ultimately brings about changes in the broader money supply measures. The blue line shows the sharp increase in reserve balances, which began in mid September 2008. For the week ending September 10, banks and other depository institutions held $8 billion in reserve balances at the Fed. By the week ending December 31, 2008, they held $848 billion. The Fed had increased the supply of reserve balances by 100-fold in just sixteen weeks.

Note also how large this increase is compared with the then-extraordinary increase in reserves around the time of 9/11, when there was physical damage to the financial markets. Then there was a clear increase in the demand for reserves, and the Fed beautifully supplied them. I remember this event well, because I was working in the U.S. Treasury at the time and Don Kohn came over and kindly shared the reserves data with me. We sat and looked at that amazing increase, and I said things like, "Wow, you guys did a terrific job" and we went on and on for about an hour. We had never seen anything like it before. That huge increase now looks like a little blip compared with where the Fed is today.

The current increase in reserves is not due to an increase in demand for reserves as on 9/11. It came about as a direct result of the Fed's decision to purchase securities and make loans to certain sectors and financial institutions. More specifically, the

Fed financed these securities purchases and loans by creating reserve balances—creating money. That is why I used the term *mondustrial* policy when I was asked to examine and explain this complex combination of monetary policy and industrial policy to those not familiar with monetary matters or with the details of the Fed's balance sheet (see Taylor 2009b).[1] Later the Federal Reserve labeled this policy credit easing (see Bernanke 2009), but perhaps a more specific term, such as *selective* credit easing, would be a better description, because expansion of the Fed's balance sheet always leads to credit easing in some form.

The Fed can obtain additional funds to finance its purchases of securities and lending in three other ways. The U.S. Treasury can borrow the funds and deposit them at the Fed. Or the Fed can borrow the funds itself by issuing debt. The Fed can also adjust the composition of its own portfolio, by selling shorter term government securities to make room for more private securities, loans, or longer term government securities.

For the first thirteen months of the financial crisis, until the week of September 10, 2008, the Fed adjusted the composition of its portfolio by selling government securities and using the funds to increase loans to depository institutions through its Term Auction Facility, to provide loans to investment banks through its Primary Dealer Credit Facility, or to purchase private assets such as those in the Bear Stearns intervention. By simply adjusting its asset portfolio, it kept reserve balances from increasing. However, starting in September, the Fed apparently decided it did not have enough government securities left in its portfolio to sell without interfering with its operations or disrupting

---

1. A list of the major private securities and loan programs is found Table 1, which is drawn from Taylor (2009b).

other programs. Hence, the Fed resorted to the money creation to finance its purchases and loans. In addition, the Treasury borrowed and deposited funds at the Fed. For this purpose the Fed created a special account where the Treasury deposited the funds; that account has now diminished, and reserve creation has had the main financing role.

Figure 1 shows that the actual level of reserve balances came down early this year, but has increased again and now exceeds the level reached at the end of 2008. The decrease came about during the period when some facilities—such as discount

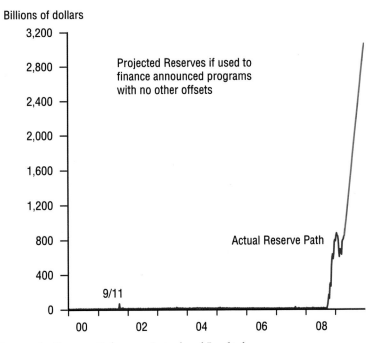

FIGURE 1. Reserve Balances: Actual and Implied

The blue line shows the actual path and the red line shows the implied future path based on policies announced by the Federal Reserve and the actual balance sheet as of April 22.

window borrowings and loans to primary dealers—were drawn down while new ones—such as mortgage-backed securities purchases—were slowly being put into operation.

Figure 1 also shows the implied increase in reserve balances (red line) if the currently announced additional purchases are to be financed by creating reserve balances and there is no other offset. This is not a forecast but rather an implication of the practice of continuing to finance by money creation the purchases of the size already announced. The large increase to around $3 trillion is due to the recently announced plans to expand the purchases of securities backed by consumer and business loans as well as the program to buy longer term Treasury securities.

The Explosion Drove the Federal Funds Rate Down to Zero

It is important to understand that the policy of increasing reserves by large amounts as shown in Figure 1 started when the federal funds interest rate target was still 2 percent, well above zero. This is demonstrated in Figure 2, which shows the start on the increase in reserves and the effective federal funds rate that was trading in the market. Some say that the reason for the explosion of reserves was that the interest rate was already at zero and could not go lower; thus the Fed had to resort to these other measures. But this is obviously incorrect.

The decline in the federal funds rate to zero followed the expansion of reserves. Indeed, judging by the timing in Figure 2, the decline in the interest rate toward the zero percent lower bound was likely caused by the expansion in reserves rather than the expansion being the inevitable result of the interest rate being at zero. The FOMC decision to lower the target for

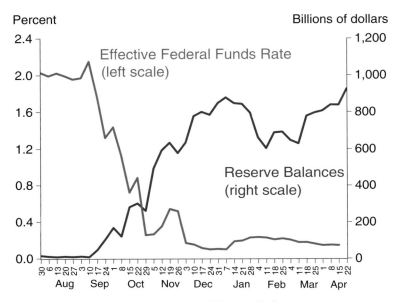

FIGURE 2. The Federal Funds Rate and Reserve Balances

the federal funds rate followed the declines in the effective federal funds rate in the market, essentially ratifying them. Clearly the increase in reserves did not start because the interest rate was at zero, but rather because of the need to finance securities purchases and loans.

REVERSING THE EXPLOSION SHOULD BE THE CENTERPIECE OF THE EXIT STRATEGY

For these reasons, reversing the increase in reserve balances should be a key part of the exit strategy to a traditional monetary policy in which a positive interest rate can be adjusted in order to maintain inflation and output stability. By adjusting reserve balances, the Trading Desk at the New York Fed affects the federal funds rate, a process I originally learned from visiting Peter Fisher and his staff at the New York Fed when he was head of the Trading Desk. By adjusting reserves, the Trading Desk moves the funds rate to where the Federal Open Market Committee wants it to be. The process is complicated because other factors also affect the federal funds rate, including expectations of future monetary actions, other short-term interest rates, and unpredictable changes in other factors supplying reserves. In fact, at the start of the crisis, the volatility of the effective funds rate increased.

In any case, assuming that the federal funds market continues to work as it has in the past, the Fed will have to bring reserve balances back down to where they were when the interest rate was last positive if it is again to have a significantly positive federal funds rate.[2] For example, if the Fed wants to have a 2 percent federal funds rate, the experience last fall suggests that it will likely have to bring the level of reserves back to what they were before the explosion in September 2008. And this means going to the lower blue line in Figure 1. In other words, assuming the Fed increases reserves by the amount shown in the red line in Figure 1, it will have to remove around three trillion dollars from the balance sheet. Before considering the difficulties in doing this, and whether there are alternatives, let us consider the timing and preparation for the exit.

---

2. I consider the issue of paying interest on reserves below.

DETERMINING WHEN TO EXIT

One way to determine when to exit is to use standard monetary policy rules. If such rules are to characterize policy after the exit from the current regime (as they did during the period of good economic performance in the 1980s and 1990s), then they can serve as a natural guideline for exiting. For example, if policy rules say that the interest rate should be raised above zero at a particular date, or a particular time interval, then that is when the Fed should exit.

One could use the Taylor rule for this purpose. Indeed, Don Kohn mentioned the Taylor rule in this context during the discussion at the Workshop on March 30, thereby informally suggesting that it might be used this way. He also mentioned that this rule called for a minus 5 percent interest rate, which implies that a positive interest rate is still pretty far off.

However, as I see it, the Taylor rule does not generate a minus 5 percent interest rate at this time. The Taylor rule says that the interest rate should be one and a half times the inflation rate plus a half times the GDP gap plus one. Whether you average a broad-based GDP inflation index over the past year, as I originally suggested, or whether you use core inflation rates, the inflation rate is not less than 1 percent at this time. It looks closer to 2 percent. The GDP gap seems to be around minus 4 percent. If you plug those numbers into the rule, you get 1½ times 2, plus ½ times −4, plus 1, which equals 2 percent. This result is not even negative, let alone minus 5 percent. And if you want to take a lower inflation rate, say 1 percent, or a somewhat bigger GDP gap, you can bring that down to close to zero, but you still don't see minus 5 percent. So this type of index does not give much basis for assuming we have a long way to go before the Fed has to raise the rate. We don't know what will happen in the future, but it is not so clear that the Fed has a long time before interest rates have to be higher. Some in the markets are already expecting rate increases next year, but time will tell.

PREPARING TO EXIT

Until the time comes to begin raising interest rates, there are several actions the Fed can take to be prepared. Some of these actions help put the FOMC in the mode of a monetary authority even though it is not voting to adjust the interest rate.

1. Focus on the Quantity of Reserves or Other Aggregates

Decisions about monetary policy can start to shift to quantities like the quantity of money or reserves rather than have those quantities solely determined by the selective credit decisions. A traditional monetary policy framework of the kind discussed widely before interest rate guidelines became popular was to focus on the level or the growth rate of the quantity of a monetary aggregate. The decisions would be about what is the appropriate growth rate of money for dealing with the recession and helping the recovery from recession. If an increase in money growth is called for, then monetary policy would bring this about by open market operations. An increase in base money would then increase the growth rate of a monetary aggregate. Of course, this is not the type of policy that is in place at this time. Rather, policy is driven by intervention into particular markets with the amount of base money growth determined by the amount of this intervention. The increase in M1 or M2 is determined by that reserve growth and by how much banks decide to hold as excess reserves. So far the banks have held a large amount of the increase in reserves, though there has been a marked increase in the growth rate of currency, demand deposits, and M1.

Currently the only broad quantitative statement by the Federal Open Market Committee is that it will keep the size of its balance sheet "at a high level for some time" (see minutes of the January 27–28 meeting in FOMC 2009). That seems too vague. Does it mean the scenario like the red line in Figure 1? Or does it mean that reserves will stay where they are now? Instead, or in conjunction with its credit decisions, the FOMC could give ranges for the growth of reserve balances, base money, and even broader monetary aggregates. The Federal Reserve staff could study the impact of various growth rates for the quantity of reserve balances or the money supply, and the FOMC could discuss and vote on these quantities, until it is time for the interest rate to go above zero. Right now we do not know the intent of the Fed or even what the contingency plan is for reversing the explosion in reserves.

There are other reasons to focus more on the level or the growth rate of money, even central bank money. The enormous increase in reserves is viewed by many as inflationary. With the economy in a recession, inflation is not now a problem, but at some time the Federal Reserve will have to remove these reserves or we will have a big inflation. Recall that increases in money growth affect inflation with a long lag. The question is whether the Fed will be able to reduce the reserves in time and whether people will expect the Fed to do so. If reserves get to the level shown by the red line in Figure 1, it will have to sell a huge amount of securities backed by consumer credit, mortgages, student loans, and auto loans. This will be difficult to do politically.

2. *Close Down Some of the New Credit Facilities Now*

Another preparatory step would be start closing down some loan or securities purchasing facilities. It is not clear how effective these interventions are, and they may be counterproductive. Certainly not all of them are working well, and some work better than others. Though the Federal Reserve has argued that all these actions are necessary because of the financial crisis and many in the financial markets agree, I have found that, for example, the Term Auction Facility had no noticeable impact on interest rate spreads. I have a concern that such actions prolonged the crisis by not addressing the fundamental problem of counterparty risk in the banks. At the least the Fed should increase its policy evaluation work in this area and create a priority list of which programs can be closed. Recently the Fed has started buying medium-term Treasuries to drive their rates down. Much of the initial announcement effect on rates has been lost already, and that is what most economic theories of the term structure tell us. Maybe the Fed could close that new facility down.

3. *Improve Transparency*

Another preparatory move is to be more transparent. I have urged more transparency about the Federal Reserve's balance sheet and its new operations, mentioning for example the need for daily data (see Taylor 2007, 2008). I am very encouraged that the Fed has created a web page to explain its new programs and its balance sheet. The Fed has also clarified some of the line items such as "other Federal Reserve assets" which had contained loans to other central banks. And the Fed has published long-term inflation forecasts that are similar to inflation targets. The Joint Treasury-Fed statement of March 23, 2009, was also aimed at clarifying roles as well as the interaction between the Fed and the Treasury in these unusual times (see Treasury Department and Federal Reserve 2009).

But there is still more that can be done. Here are five suggestions:

- It would still be useful if daily, rather than only weekly, balance sheet data were provided. This is very important as the exit strategy begins, but even historical data with a month or two lag would be helpful.
- It also would be helpful to publish more detailed minutes of Federal Reserve Board meetings where decisions that affect the Fed's balance sheet or the quantity of reserves are made. There is no reason why these cannot be as detailed as the minutes of the FOMC meetings and released in a timely fashion.
- The Fed should release the results of their evaluation studies of the facilities.
- If the Fed does use a monetary policy rule to determine the time of exit, then it should be transparent about the rule.
- While the March 23 Joint Fed-Treasury statement provides clarity, it is missing a key phrase that was in the 1951 Accord between the Treasury and the Fed: the part pertaining to the *monetization of the debt*. The Accord announced on March 4, 1951, by the Secretary of the Treasury, the Chairman of the Fed, and the FOMC stated:

"The Treasury and the Federal Reserve System have reached full accord with respect to debt management and monetary policies to be pursued in furthering their common purpose to assure the successful financing of the Government's requirements and, at the same time, to minimize monetization of the public debt." With the large amount of borrowing by the Treasury now scheduled, a mention of the principle of avoiding monetization would be valuable.

ALTERNATIVES TO SELLING ASSETS?

Now let me briefly consider other ways that have been suggested to provide the Fed with the power to set the short-term interest rate without selling off $3 trillion in assets.

1. Increasing the Interest Rate Paid on Reserves

One such suggestion is to continue to pay interest on reserves and to raise that interest rate once a higher federal funds rate is called for. One problem with this approach, however, is that it was tried last fall and did not work. When reserve balances increased last fall, the federal funds rate dropped to zero very fast even though interest was paid on reserves near the federal funds rate target set by the FOMC. This phenomenon surprised the Fed staff and many others. There have been several possible explanations, such as that banks did not want to be seen to be exploiting the obvious arbitrage opportunity, but none are fully satisfactory, and more study of that period is necessary before we can rely on this approach method.

Another problem with this approach is the large payments to the banks, which will be difficult to justify. To get an understanding for the magnitudes involved, consider this example. If reserve balances stay at $3,000 billion and the equilibrium interest rate is 4 percent, then the Fed will be paying banks $120 billion per year, year after year.

2. *Absorbing Balances Through Fed or Treasury Borrowing*

Another possibility is to take actions to absorb the reserves either by (i) issuing Federal Reserve debt or (ii) having the Treasury borrow and deposit funds at the Fed. The former was actually mentioned in the March 23 Joint Fed-Treasury statement and the latter has already been used, so these are not hypothetical suggestions. However, while these ideas do help with monetary base control, they raise worrisome independence issues for the Fed. The danger I see is that as the recovery begins, or after we are a couple of years into it, people may feel that it's not fast enough, or there is an unpleasant pause. Either could generate heavy pressure on the Fed to intervene in the mortgage market or in some other market. In fact, you could imagine that the Federal Reserve becomes the permanent selective credit agency, borrowing funds in one market and allocating it to other markets. Why would such interventions only take place in times of crisis? Why wouldn't future Fed officials use them to try to make economic expansions stronger or to assist certain sectors and industries for other reasons?

If we are to have a selective credit policy with the inherent credit risks involved, I believe it is more appropriate for the Treasury or some other agency of the executive branch to take it on with the approval of the Congress with the purposes stated and debated transparently. What justification is there for an independent government agency to engage in such a selective credit policy? For the Federal Reserve to be taking on these responsibilities raises questions about its independence. The recent request by the Treasury for the Fed to assist in creating a Consumer and Business Loan Initiative is reminiscent of the request by Treasury for the Fed to help out in its borrowing operations before the Accord of 1951. Thus, giving the Fed the authority to borrow to finance these extraordinary measures has the potential to change the role of the central bank in ways that could be harmful. The success of monetary policy during the great moderation period of long expansions and mild recessions was not due to a lot of discretion but to following predictable policies and guidelines that worked.

For these reasons, the best exit strategy is to reduce the amount of reserve to levels consistent with a traditional interest rate rule without giving the Fed the authority to borrow for credit allocation purposes and without relying solely on paying interest on reserves. Now is the time to prepare for the strategy and to clarify as transparently as possible the guidelines under which it will operate.

REFERENCES

Bernanke, Ben (2009), "The Crisis and the Policy Response," The Stamp Lecture, London School of Economics, London, England, Jan. 13.

FOMC (2009), "Minutes of the Federal Open Market Committee," Washington, DC, Jan. 27-28, available at www.federal reserve.gov/monetarypolicy/files/fomcminutes20090128.pdf.

Taylor, John B. (2007), " Housing and Monetary Policy" remarks presented at the Kansas City Federal Reserve Bank Conference in Jackson Hole, Wyoming, Aug. 31–Sept. 1.

Taylor, John B. (2008), "Monetary Policy and the State of the Economy," Testimony before the Committee on Financial Services, U.S. House of Representatives, Feb. 26.

Taylor, John B. (2009a), *Getting Off Track: How Government Actions and Interventions Caused, Prolonged, and Worsened the Financial Crisis*, Stanford, CA: Hoover Institution Press.

Taylor, John B. (2009b), "The Need to Return to a Monetary Framework," Prepared for the National Association of Business Economics Panel, "Long-Run Economic Challenges: A Federal Reserve Perspective," San Francisco, Jan. 3 and forthcoming in *Business Economics*, Vol. 43, No 2.

Treasury Department and Federal Reserve (2009), Joint Statement on "The Role of the Federal Reserve in Preserving Financial and Monetary Stability," press release issued Mar. 23, available at www.federalreserve.gov/newsevents/press/monetary/20090323b.htm.

Part III:

Paving the Way with Market and Regulatory Reforms

7

MARKET-BASED MECHANISMS TO REDUCE SYSTEMIC RISK

Myron S. Scholes

With the advent of the financial/economic crisis of 2008, financial entities, corporations, consumers, investors, and governments need to reduce debt, whether in the United States, Europe, Asia, or in emerging market countries. Asset values have fallen dramatically as risk premiums have increased, and the income-generating potential of assets has fallen. If asset values continue to fall, entities must continue to reduce leverage. With falls in asset values, debtors must issue equity, sell assets, or rely on external guarantees to provide cash to pay down or support debt and reduce risk. The cost of issuing equity, of selling assets, or relying on guarantees, however, becomes extreme at times of shock. Credit markets cease to function efficiently.

What regulations or new market-based mechanisms should we implement to reduce the potential impact or the import of systemic shocks going forward? To answer this question, I first set the stage by discussing some of the key determinants of risk in the financial markets. I then propose ways in which market players and central banks, including the Federal Reserve, can help to reduce those risks.

CAPITAL STRUCTURE ISSUES: VOLATILITY, LEVERAGE, AND RISK

The risks to individual financial firms and the financial system are functions of a number of variables, including volatility and leverage. Understanding how these factors affect risk and vulnerability is the first step to designing appropriate market-based mechanisms to deal with them.

The Role of Volatility

In a perfect market, Franco Modigliani and Merton Miller proved over fifty years ago that the value of the firm is not enhanced by using more debt (see Modigliani and Miller 1958). Although the expected return on equity increases with more debt, the risk increases just enough to offset the value of increased expected returns. Financial entities that increase their expected return on equity by increasing leverage do not add value for their stockholders.

When volatility is low, increasing leverage to increase equity volatility to a target volatility level—and thereby enhance expected returns—comes at the cost of greater risk. And, many financial entities do target volatility to keep up with competitors that also increase leverage when volatility is low. Unfortunately, if future volatility turns out to be unexpectedly greater than forecast, adjustment costs to reduce risk in this new environment become extremely high. The deadweight costs incurred to sell assets, to raise cash, and to reduce leverage to reduce risk are extremely high.

Regulators should not allow financial entities to reduce their equity capital based on notions that economic volatility is lower and will remain so. More equity capital is good. And, central bankers and regulators should not encourage leverage by making statements to the effect that mini shocks should be ignored and "that the fundamentals of the economy are strong." Market participants believe that central bankers have information that they do not have and incorporate this information, whether signaled to them through interest rate changes or public statements. If central bankers attempt to dampen natural market volatility, the unintended consequences of these short-term actions will be to encourage leverage and other forms of risk taking. For example, "we will increase interest rates at a measured pace." The adjustment costs in the aftermath will be far greater.

By way of an analogy, for many years, firefighters put out every small fire in Yellowstone National Park and other areas of the western United States. The underbrush grew, setting the stage for multiple lightning strikes to cause fires to destroy much greater areas in the park than if fires initially had been left to burn of their own accord. Financial regulators do the same thing when they dampen volatility; they put out small fires but encourage risk-taking and thus increase the likelihood of a major conflagration. We don't know the level of volatility in the economy that balances the need for more risk taking to enhance returns (the underbrush grows) and the cost of adjustment at times of shock (lightning striking many parts of the park). But, low volatility is not necessarily the norm to avoid the consequences of shocks in the growth of the economy.

We need to trade off the benefits of "mini-shocks" causing natural market adjustments through price changes, unemployment, and business failures with the costs of dampening these effects and a possible follow-on "mega-shock." And, like Yellowstone National Park, the effects are non-linear. The costs of adjustment to a mega shock may be multiples of the summation of the costs of adjustment to mini-shocks. And, the costs of adjustment to mini-shocks most likely won't involve the central bank or the treasury.

Challenges in Reducing Leverage

Leverage is a reduced form measure of risk; that is, two firms with the same leverage ratio might have far different equity risks, because the risk of underlying assets supporting each firm's debt is different. However, leverage theory does not take into account that entities must act to reduce risk, and to act is costly. Leverage reduction does not happen on its own. As the value of assets supporting the debt falls, the risk of the equity increases if the entity does not take explicit actions to reduce risk. Under the form of contracting currently in place, to reduce risk is extremely expensive, because most financial entities are interconnected: latent risk factors affect them simultaneously, and many must reduce risk at the same time.

Financial entities find that at times of shock, the cost to issue equity capital is extremely high. Most of the value of the capital raised is transferred to the benefit of debt holders at the expense of the equity holders. Debt holders are made better off when more equity is raised to support their claims. Therefore, equity holders are unable or unwilling to add to equity, for they recognize that to reduce risk through issuing equity destroys its value. The more equity that is raised, the lower the value of existing equity. By issuing equity, equity holders reduce the value of their option to pay off the debt in the future (for example, see Black and Scholes 1973). This has been labeled the "debt trap."

Moreover, at times of shock, debt covenants preclude financial entities from issuing senior debt. Debt holders had contracted to retain their senior claims on assets. To change the form of debt contracts and reduce constraints at times of crisis is expensive. When central bankers support financial entities, debt holders are "bailed out." The financial entity has more assets to support their claims.

Financial entities profit by making markets in and holding inventories of less liquid assets, such as: (1) loans to corporations, investors, other financial entities, (2) mortgage contracts and mortgage structures, (3) guarantees such as lines of credit, stable-value products, and other financing arrangements, (4) derivative contracts including interest rate swaps and credit default swaps, and (5) other structured products, including so-called "Collateralized Debt Obligations" containing mixtures of subprime mortgages, student loans, and credit-card loans. The inventory holdings generally have a longer maturity period than the liabilities used to finance them. Financial entities earn a liquidity premium and a risk premium on their inventory holdings as long as they are able to hold and finance their inventory.

The liquidity premium, however, does not remain constant. With mini- and mega-shocks, the price of liquidity increases as financial entities no longer are willing to act as a principal to inventory these securities and, as a result, reduce their provision of liquidity. They no longer have confidence in their model values, how extreme prices might become because of market flows, their ability to transfer inventory risk, and for how long they might need to hold onto their inventory before they are able to sell at a profit to earn a return on capital employed. As a result, they stop intermediating risk. They no longer perform the classical speculator function in markets.

At times of shock, other investors wish to sell risky assets and move to safer, more liquid securities such as government bonds. Financial entities follow other investors and attempt to sell assets to reduce risk. As they and other investors demand liquidity from the market, the price of liquidity increases. Time stops. Calendar time and decision time become disjointed. Increasing volatility forces market participants to make decisions extremely quickly, which is often impossible to do in times of shock. Time is needed for speculators to recalibrate or reformulate their models to restore their ability to intermediate.

At extremes, participants in the dealer markets are able to transact sporadically and at wide spreads. And, financial entities might be unable to refinance their short-term debt, causing additional liquidations. Potential investors do not know to what extent asset values are lower because of increases in the price of liquidity or because asset values have fallen. Therefore, a leveraged market-making business is inherently unstable. Banks might be the wrong providers of liquidity to markets. Simply put, leverage can only be reduced by selling assets to raise cash if market makers are making markets in the assets they need to sell and they no longer can continue to do so at times of shock and to make conditions worse, they borrow from each other with short-term financing to hold longer-maturity, relatively idiosyncratic assets.

MARKET-BASED SOLUTIONS TO REDUCE RISKS AND MITIGATE ADJUSTMENT COSTS AT TIMES OF SHOCK

Market-based measures are needed to manage the risks and vulnerabilities discussed above and to make the financial system more reslient to shocks.

The Need to Move Risks to Markets

The solution to the market-making paradox—small returns most of the time, big losses occasionally at times of market shock (that might have to be borne by taxpayers through "bailouts")—is to move as much risk as possible to markets and away from financial entities. During this crisis, equity prices on exchanges fell by approximately fifty percent. These markets functioned extremely well, because these are not leveraged markets. Buyers and sellers were able to come together through market price discovery mechanisms. Government bond markets and interest rate swap markets functioned as expected. Nearly all other credit markets, whether leveraged dealer or over-the-counter markets, failed to function with any degree of efficiency.

This being said, the problem is to distinguish risks that can be migrated to markets from those that must be kept to make markets. Holding excess inventory to earn a liquidity premium, a premium that is magnified through leverage makes financial entities more exposed to shocks. With the costs of computers and telecommunications technology far lower today than 5 years ago, 10 years ago, etc., the cost to migrate risks to markets must be a fraction of what it once was.

Yet, financial entities profit from making money on the bid-offer spreads and resist moving these securities to electronic exchanges, where spreads and liquidity premiums will come down. Financial entities enjoy earning the liquidity premium on holding inventory, the small steady returns, and, therefore, carry far more inventory than needed to manage their market-making activities (because of moral hazard and incentive issues within organizations). And, there are insufficient data to distinguish whether the inventory premium is a liquidity premium (a payment for providing liquidity) or a shock premium (making money most of the time and losing it all occasionally).

It is ironic that those screaming to eliminate mark-to-market accounting don't realize that doing so exacerbates the inventory problem because financial entities have the incentive to retain and add more illiquid assets on their books where losses can be hidden through the opacity of holding assets at original purchase price or for resale or marking assets by those models supplied by the desks that are suffering the losses in the first place.

The Problem with Fed Guarantees

One priority must be to reduce the adverse effects of central bank guarantees, which can induce market players to assume excessive risk.

Debt holders expect to be "bailed-out" at times of shock. Lower debt-to-equity ratios—more capital to support asset positions—lowers the value of the implicit guarantee for a given volatility of the returns on the underlying assets and reduces the expectation of the dead-weight costs of using the guarantees at times of shock. The Fed and other central banks will have to establish a risk monitoring system that anticipates that financial entities confronted with the need for increased equity to support positions will attempt to increase risk to enhance the value of the guarantees.

Establishing a uniform global risk management system through the auspices of the Bank for International Settlements is not the correct approach. The agreed solution will take years to implement and will become a watered-down version of what is needed to manage risk. A case in point here is the value-at-risk framework (so-called "VaR") and the framework that allows banks to set their own risk management systems to determine their own equity capital requirements. The risk management system should require risk capital based on shocks and not on correlations such as a VaR calculation. Correlations are conditional means. Means are impossible to estimate accurately. At times of shock, we know that diversification breaks down because liquidity prices change together increasing the observed correlations.

Central bankers should require capital for each asset class based on shocks and ignore any correlations or offsets. This would increase equity capital requirements uniformly across financial entities. A uniform shock-based-capital system would mitigate the need for one financial entity to increase risk to earn a higher rate of return on equity to keep up with another competitor that had increased risk.

When shocks hit, the cost of central bank guarantees can be tremendous. For example, the amount of asset write-downs needed in the crisis of 2008 requires a gigantic recapitalization of financial entities around the world, somewhat in excess of $4 trillion. This is not politically feasible. The standard ways in which governments politically recapitalize the banking system entail:

(1) programs, each one seeming small, but in aggregate adding up to a large hidden cost as central banks buy illiquid assets from banks at above market prices claiming that markets will recover, or finance illiquid and risky positions at a lower than market rate of interest;

(2) quantitative easing programs to buy longer-dated bonds at short-term inflated prices from the banks;

(3) restricting competition through regulations such that customers pay higher fees and obtain less competitive services;

(4) unrealistic accounting assumptions to provide time for asset prices to recover hoping that lack of liquidity was the problem; and

(5) bailing out bond holders so they continue to finance bank activities.

These protracted methods are politically easier to implement than direct recapitalization but still have a cost. For example, the Bank of Japan took many years to recapitalize the banking system to rebuild profits through a zero interest-rate policy, excess reserve policy, and through quantitative easing.

The Importance of Stronger Derivatives Markets

Another key issue is to develop market-based mechanisms to strengthen the derivatives markets. When shocks occur, over-the-counter dealer markets do not function, because intermediaries reduce or eliminate inventory positions and act only as an agent. Many other investment pools, such as hedge funds, need to sell assets to reduce risk and leverage and to meet investor withdrawal requests. To facilitate transactions, markets need price signals. As stated, it is cost effective to quote bids and offers on electronic exchanges. This will help to bring buyers and sellers together efficiently. Currently, last sales for small orders are posted on a system called TRACE. However, those prices may be far from current markets and prices available for large-scale transacting.

Financial entities resist moving price quotes for derivative products like CDS, ABS, RMBS, and CMBS to electronic exchanges because they benefit from the lack of transparency in non-shock times and in the short-term earn large market-making profits in shock periods as other entities reduce their risks. For example, the large profits in fixed-income trading reported by such banks as J.P. Morgan and Goldman Sachs during the first three months of 2009 resulted from fixed-income activities at the expense of clients who needed to reduce risk in a bilateral market.

The Fed's support of particular financial entities enabled them to charge large liquidation fees to the non-supported hedge funds, pension funds, and corporate clients. Consideration should be given to an analysis of the unintended consequences and costs of bailouts of particular financial entities. The net result might be to reduce competition in the markets, thereby increasing monopoly profits for some at the expense of other market participants.

Moreover, if all CDS (and other derivative contracts) can be closed out at mid-market prices, market participants would be able to unwind contracts at times of shock without paying large bid-offer spreads. Once a CDS contract becomes a standardized instrument, future transactions should migrate to a clearing corporation of the variety discussed by Darrell Duffie in this volume (see also Duffie and Zhu 2009). This will not only provide contract information and exchange pricing but also enable regulators to monitor the trading activities of market participants using inside information to their advantage. A clearing corporation reduces the costs of liquidation of risks. It cannot handle, however, idiosyncratic, non-standardized contracts.

All dealers and market participants should be required to post initial margins on derivative contracts (e.g., AIG did not post initial margins on its guarantees (CDS contracts)). The Fed and other central banks should study the effects of margin, credit markets, liquidity provision, and their policies on the operation of markets. A clearing corporation is an institution that might help.

Alternatives to Fed Guarantees

We must take measures to reduce the value of government guarantees and the need for costly government intervention. As the preceding discussion has suggested, there are many routes to achieve this result:

(1) The Fed and other regulators could require more equity capital, reducing the probability of default and the call on a government guarantee.

(2) The Federal Reserve could use the credit default swap market or the differential between Libor rates and Federal Funds rates to estimate premiums that it would charge each period to provide guarantees.

(3) Banks could be required to leverage their operations through only using convertible debt. This convertible debt must be converted into a predetermined fraction of the equity of the financial entity on a systemic event, either declared by the central bank or by a fall in the market value of a bank index, or both. As a result, the

bank immediately has additional equity and does not need to sell assets to raise capital in illiquid markets at potentially "fire sale" prices. And, since bank debt holders are not bailed out by a central bank, this greatly reduces the "moral hazard" problem. Debt holders will be more cautious and more cognizant of the amount of on- and off-balance sheet bank leverage. Moreover, there is more certainty as to the terms of the actual bank debt contract in the event of a market shock wherein renegotiation of contracts is a further deadweight cost to the system. In this crisis some debt holders were "bailed out," others suffered losses. This solution reduces the value of government guarantees, eliminates the "debt trap" problem, and limits the risk of assets held in inventory. (See an independent cut at this in Squam Lake Working Group 2009.)

(4) The Fed could grant guarantees only on investments that are one-hundred percent backed by actual government debt. For example, money market funds should not offer stable-value products or banks should not offer floating-rate short-term preferred stock. Insurance companies should not offer annuities that provide a minimum return while at the same time investing investor proceeds in risky instruments that promise higher returns. Savings deposits at banks should be invested in government bonds if they are offered as stable-value products. Bank market-making activities should be funded in the credit markets with convertible debt as described above. The bank needs to separate itself into at least two banks, one a money market bank and, the other an investment bank.

(5) Contingent capital arrangements should be encouraged. Financial entities should pay other entities such as pension funds or insurance companies an annual fee for the right to draw capital to support their activities. If the cost of this contingent capital is too great, correctly so, financial entities will reduce their risk-taking activities. These contingent-capital contracts internalize the costs of providing risk products and reduce the need for central bank guarantees. The central banks might compete and offer contingent capital contracts at auction each year to determine a market-based price.

(6) Any form of bank guarantee must be disclosed to regulators and to the markets. Accountants should not obfuscate these guarantees, and their economic value should be included in the financial reporting process.

(7) Derivative contracts provide both risk transfer and leverage services. These contracts are used to hedge risks. There are some who argue that credit-default swaps should only be written on those firms in which the writer has an insurable interest. This same argument extends to futures contracts such as shorting the S&P 500 futures index or taking positions in government bond futures or option contracts on indices or bonds. I believe that instead of artificial limitations on risk transfer and hedging mechanisms, better risk management and margining systems are of lower cost and greater benefit to society than restricting innovation and use of derivative contracts.

(8) Andrew Lo has suggested that as in the case of the Federal Aviation Administration, after every financial crisis (or even a financial entity failure) a board of ex-

perts and market participants should examine the causes of the failure and what to learn from it (see Lo 2008). This knowledge will not only benefit regulators in making policy choices but also market participants such as senior bank management who must make strategic decisions for their organizations.

INTERCONNECTEDNESS IN MARKETS: THE AGGREGATION PROBLEM AND A POSSIBLE ROLE FOR A SYSTEMIC RISK REGULATOR

A further set of challenges to markets and regulators surrounds the problem of interconnectedness. Each financial entity has its own myopic risk management system. It measures its risks and its needs for future adjustments based on its assumptions about the completeness of markets through its measurement and analysis of its ability to liquidate assets at times of stress. But this is an inexact science to say the least.

The problem arises when many financial entities attempt to liquidate assets concurrently to reduce risk and leverage. The information set is so vast that no financial entity knows what the simultaneous demands for liquidity might be among other financial entities in the system and what sequences will unfold. With losses, entities sell securities that are liquid and have not fallen in value. These sales, in turn, reduce their prices and liquidity there falls as well, causing the need for further sales and an increase in liquidity prices. Investors do not know whether the shock is a liquidity shock or a change in economic valuations. If the former, prices will mean-revert over time; if the latter, prices will not rebound. Obviously, a shock causes reassessment of future prospects.

Market participants must assess the future role of government as the financial crisis results in government replacing private initiatives. An example here is the Private/Public Investment Partnership (PPIP) program. Until market participants understand how "toxic" assets are to be liquidated, if at all, they will not enter the credit markets. Moreover, if the government reduces market transparency through elimination of market-based accounting measurement, the new opacity will slow down the evaluation process and inhibit market participants from making investment decisions necessary for economic recovery. Prices must find their economic levels. I am in favor of disclosure of mark-to-market valuations for investor information and to reduce opacity. Regulators, however, can decide bank capital requirements on any measure they deem appropriate.

A systemic risk regulator (Andrew Crockett and Michael Halloran use the term systemic stability regulator in their chapters in this volume) would benefit the financial system if that regulator is able to obtain information from each financial entity as to the risks they are measuring (such as sensitivities to factor risks or shock tests or scenario analysis), aggregates that information, and resends the aggregated risk information back to each of the financial entities. This aggregated information might warn a particular financial entity to reduce risk because the aggregated risk was greater than assumed. Other entities, however, might assume the opposite. Through a process of information sharing, the risk regulator could provide the risk signals that will allow the system as a whole to manage risks by taking account of the information contained in the actions and the risks of others. This aggregation process is extremely valuable to market participants.

A systemic risk regulator should lead the effort to revamp the financial reporting system to bring more risk measures into the income statements and balance sheets of financial entities. For example, balance sheets are snapshots at a moment in time, and do not provide dynamics or risk measures or the value of guarantees, incentive compensation contracts, and off balance sheet assets and liabilities. Accounting systems need to be revamped to handle derivatives and to incorporate off-balance sheet risks in other than footnotes.

A systemic risk regulator, however, will have no ability to micro manage the financial system or a particular financial entity. That is too tough an assignment and one that will fail. In reality, the regulator would not be able to predict or to figure out the magnitude of a "bubble" in advance. Most likely the regulator would mislead the market in that, if doing nothing, the market concluded that it was appropriate to take on additional risks.

CONCLUSION: ISSUES OF INNOVATION

Economic theory suggests that infrastructure to support financial innovation must follow that innovation. Otherwise, it would be too expensive to build all of the information links, legal rules and risk management controls, etc., in advance of new product introductions. Since successful innovations are hard to predict, infrastructure necessary to support innovation needs to lag the innovations themselves, which increases the probability that controls will be insufficient at times to prevent breakdowns in governance mechanisms. Failures, however, do not lead to the conclusion that re-regulation will succeed in stemming future failures. Or that society will be better off with fewer innovations and better off vetting innovations in advance of initiation. Although governments are able to regulate organizational forms, they are unable to regulate the services provided by competing entities, many yet unborn.

The response to this dilemma is difficult. The senior management of banks must use simple common sense tests to judge whether controls are adequate and when more resources should be placed on infrastructure. Senior management or a senior management team should understand financial engineering. The time has long gone where the leadership of financial entities should reside in the hands of those who do not understand markets or the products and risks that their entities offer to the markets. Board members of financial entities should understand risk reports, financial results, and be able to demand and understand clear explanations of the risks.

We must realize that shocks are a necessary part of growth and innovation. Financial entities are always striving to innovate to provide more efficient mechanisms to facilitate transacting, to finance larger-scale investments, to save for the future, to transfer and share risks, to provide pricing signals, and to reduce information asymmetries. We must foster innovation and attempt to internalize the costs of innovation within the financial system.

REFERENCES

Black, Fischer and Myron Scholes (1973), "The Pricing of Options and Corporate Liabilities," *Journal of Political Economy*, vol. 81, pp. 637–654.

Duffie, Darrell and Haoxiang Zhu (2009). "Does a Central Clearing Counterparty Reduce Counterpary Risk?" Stanford University Working Paper, Mar. 9.

Lo, Andrew (2008), "Hedge Funds, Systemic Risk, and the Financial Crisis of 2007–2008," Paper Prepared for the U.S. House of Representatives Committee on Oversight and Government Reform, Hearing on Hedge Funds, Nov. 13.

Modigliani, Franco and Merton Miller (1958), "The Cost of Capital, Corporation Finance and the Theory of Investment," *American Economic Review*, vol. 48, no. 3, pp. 261–297.

Squam Lake Working Group (2009), "An Expedited Resolution Mechanism for Distressed Financial Firms: Regulatory Hybrid Securities," Paper for the Council on Foreign Relations, Apr.

8

POLICY ISSUES FACING THE MARKET FOR CREDIT DERIVATIVES

Darrell Duffie

THE FINANCIAL CRISIS has prompted calls for revamping the market for credit derivatives. For example, in a July 2008 speech, Fed Chairman Ben Bernanke noted that, "The Federal Reserve, together with other regulators and the private sector, is engaged in a broad effort to strengthen the financial infrastructure. In doing so, we aim not only to help make the financial system better able to withstand future shocks but also—by reducing the range of circumstances in which systemic stability concerns might prompt government intervention—to mitigate moral hazard and the problem of 'too big to fail.'" His prime example was the effort "to improve arrangements for clearing and settling credit default swaps (CDS) and other OTC derivatives" (see Bernanke 2008). In this chapter, I consider several possible reforms of the infrastructure of the credit derivative markets and evaluate their potential impacts on systemic stability and transparency.

Volumes of trade in this relatively new market have exploded, doubling more or less every year for the past decade, and placing severe strains on market infrastructure. Some commentators have expressed severe concerns over counterparty risk and a perceived lack of market transparency. This chapter focuses on several related policy initiatives, the most significant of which is clearing.

A CDS is a contract providing insurance against losses that may occur if a named borrower defaults. The buyer of protection makes periodic payments, analogous to insurance premiums, at a contractual "CDS rate." For example, a CDS rate of 200 basis points means that for each year until the named borrower defaults, the buyer of protection pays a premium of 2% of the principal amount of debt covered by the contract. This principal amount is called the "notional" CDS position. At the default of the named borrower, the seller of protection pays the difference between the principal amount of debt insured and the market value of the debt. For example, on a notional CDS position of $100 million, if default brings the market value of a corporation's debt down to 40 cents on the dollar, the seller of protection would pay $60 million to the buyer of protection.

At its default, Lehman's senior unsecured debt recovery was about 8 cents on the dollar, for a protection payment of 92 cents per notional dollar. All scheduled Lehman CDS protection claims were paid, according to data from the Depository Trust and Clearing Corporation (DTCC). In general, there have been no known significant failures of CDS protection sellers to make good on their promises.

Credit default swaps are traded over the counter, rather than on an exchange. That is, each contract is negotiated privately between two counterparties. At the end of 2008, default swaps covered $38.6 trillion of debt principal, according to data provided by the International Swaps and Derivatives Association (ISDA). The majority of these positions, however, are in the form of dealer-to-dealer CDS positions, because of the role of dealers as market intermediaries.

Proposals to reduce systemic risk and to provide additional transparency in the credit derivatives market have focused on clearing and on exchange trading. I will briefly address these and related policy issues. My general conclusion is that, thanks in part to the efforts of the New York Federal Reserve, the markets for credit default swaps are more transparent and safer than they were several years ago. More could be done to improve safety and price transparency. The advent of clearing for the CDS market, although a positive development in principle, has had some unintended adverse consequences that could be corrected by reducing the number of clearing houses and by simultaneously clearing CDS positions along with other types of over-the-counter derivatives, as I will explain. I also believe that the regulatory framework of the insurance industry, at least in its current form, is not suitable for credit derivatives. I make a proposal to improve price transparency in the over-the-counter market for credit derivatives.

IMPROVEMENTS TRIGGERED BY THE NEW YORK FEDERAL RESERVE BANK

Regulators, most importantly the New York Federal Reserve Bank, have feared that dealers, which are systemically important financial institutions, could suffer debilitating losses as a result of their CDS positions. Beginning in 2005, the New York Fed put significant pressure on dealers to better document their trades in order to mitigate the risk that dealers would be unable to determine the extent of their exposures to each other in the event of a major default. Eventually, the DTCC established a "trade information warehouse" that now captures the majority of information on CDS trades covering corporate and sovereign borrowers. Although the trade details are private information, the DTCC now provides weekly data on the aggregate amount of CDS protection written on approximately 1,000 of these borrowers, adding a measure of transparency to the market. Were it not for the major improvements in documentation that were prompted by the actions of the New York Fed, it is plausible that the failure of Lehman would have caused significant confusion over settlement obligations, leading to severe additional counterparty risk and even counterparty failures. In actuality, the settlement of default claims on Lehman CDS was a relatively routine operation, without a single reported counterparty failure.

In another move to reduce systemic risk in the CDS market, the New York Fed has pressed dealers to have their trades cleared. Once two counterparties agree on the terms of a credit default swap, they can "clear" the CDS by having a central clearing counterparty, commonly known as a "clearing house," stand between them, acting as the buyer of protection to one counterparty and the seller of protection to the other. The original counterparties are thus insulated from direct exposure to each other's default, and rely instead on the performance of the clearing house.

Clearing can in principle reduce counterparty exposures because it allows positive and negative counterparty exposures to be netted against each other more easily. For example, suppose that Dealer A has bought CDS protection on $100 million notional amount of debt from Dealer B. Suppose that Dealer B has an identical position as buyer of protection on a credit default swap with Dealer C, who in turn has the same position as buyer of protection on a CDS with Dealer A. All three dealers are exposed to a counterparty default. That circle of exposures could be eliminated by clearing all three trades through the same clearing house. Because of the opportunity to net long against short positions, and because in this simple example each dealer is long and short by the same amount, the clearing house and the three dealers would have no risk at all.

The failure of the dealer community to develop central clearing of CDS positions before this year may have been due to the cost and complexity of setting up an effective clearing house, and to the fact that individual dealers do not fully internalize the benefits of systemic risk reduction. The systemic-risk externality associated with large-dealer derivatives exposures leaves some scope for regulatory intervention. The U.S. Treasury Department has announced that, in the future, clearing will be required for all credit default swaps whose contractual terms are sufficiently standard.

Counterparties typically post collateral with their counterparties, including clearing houses, as a form of margin against their contractual obligations. According to data from ISDA, about two-thirds of CDS positions are collateralized. The amount of collateral to be posted against a CDS position is normally adjusted with changes in the market value of the position. For example, if the estimated market value of a CDS contract to the buyer of protection rises, then the seller of protection may be required to post additional collateral. Whenever clearing reduces counterparty exposures, this also typically reduces the amount of collateral that would be demanded as a form of guarantee against performance. Collateral is a scarce resource, especially during a financial crisis.

A significant reduction in CDS exposures has already occurred through "compression trades," which have the effect of terminating redundant circles of CDS positions such as those of the example described above, using a "tear-up" procedure. In such a compression trade, the several dealers involved would legally cancel their offsetting obligations to each other, settling with each other in cash for the market values of any minor differences in the original contractual terms.

Compression trades organized by TriOptima are responsible for the termination of approximately $30 trillion notional in CDS positions in 2008 alone. Largely as a result of compression trades, the aggregate notional size of the CDS market has been reduced from roughly $60 trillion in mid-2008 to about $39 trillion at this point. Central clearing can achieve reductions in counterparty exposures, beyond those available through compression trades, because, unlike compression trades, clearing does not rely merely on offsetting long and short positions on the same named borrower.

POTENTIAL UNINTENDED ADVERSE CONSEQUENCES OF CLEARING

Because any active clearing house is by nature a highly systemic financial institution, it should be extremely well capitalized and have impeccable operational controls. In normal

practice, each member of a clearing house is required to contribute to a guarantee fund that backs the performance of the
clearing house in the event that one of its members fails to perform and that member's collateral is found to be insufficient
to cover the failed position. Setting up a clearing house for derivatives also requires standardization of the derivatives to be
cleared and of the collateral requirements. Minimum standards have been proposed by the International Organization
of Securities Commissions (IOSCO). In the United States,
clearing houses are regulated by the Fed and the Commodity
Futures Trading Commission (CFTC), and operate for now
under a temporary exemption from regulation by the Securities and Exchange Commission. The first two U.S. clearing
houses were approved in 2009. One of these is operated by the
Intercontinental Exchange (ICE). Another is operated by the
Chicago Mercantile Exchange in a joint venture with Citadel,
a major hedge fund.

In addition to these two U.S. clearing houses, five more
have been set up or proposed in Europe. Unfortunately, some
of the benefits of netting described above are lost with each
additional clearing house. The efficient netting of positive
against negative exposures is difficult if some of the CDS positions of a derivatives dealer are cleared through one clearing
house and others are cleared through a different clearing
house. With sufficient standardization of contracts and collateral terms, netting across clearing houses might be feasible, but
this is not part of any existing proposals. As clearing houses
compete for market share, it is important that they do not attempt to attract business by relaxing collateral standards or
guarantee fund contributions.

Beyond the netting opportunities that are lost with more

than one CDS clearing house, there are additional lost netting opportunities whenever clearing houses are dedicated solely to credit default swaps. In addition to their CDS positions, major derivatives dealers have large positions in interest rate swaps and other types of OTC derivatives. Typically, a credit default swap is part of a master swap agreement by which the two counterparties net their aggregate bilateral exposure across all types of OTC derivatives.

For example, if Dealer A has an interest rate swap with Dealer B with a market value of $150 million in favor of Dealer A, while at the same time Dealer A has a CDS with Dealer B with a market value of $100 million in favor of Dealer B, the net exposure of Dealer A to default by Dealer B is the difference, $50 million, before considering collateral. If the two dealers clear the default swap through a CDS-dedicated clearinghouse, they cannot net their exposure from this contract against the interest rate swap exposure. As a result of clearing the CDS, the exposure of Dealer A to Dealer B would therefore rise to $150 million. The collateral that Dealer B posts to Dealer A would also rise precipitously. In addition, the clearing house is now exposed to Dealer A by $100 million, so Dealer A must now post collateral to the clearing house against that exposure. Further, Dealer B now has an exposure to the clearing house of $100 million.

Although clearing houses are likely to have relatively low default risk, clearing houses have defaulted in the past. Ensuring their safety and soundness is expensive and requires regulatory attention. The more clearing houses that are set up, the greater will be the total exposure that they pose to their counterparties, and the larger will be the number of systemically important financial institutions whose risks must be monitored by regulators.

Recent research suggests that, for the current structure of OTC markets, dedicating clearing houses to credit default swaps, only, actually *increases* average counterparty exposures when all types of over-the-counter derivatives are considered, because of the reduced opportunity to net credit derivatives exposures against other OTC derivatives exposures (see Duffie and Zhu 2009). Along with any increase in average counterparty exposure comes an increase in demands for collateral (a scarce resource) and for contributions to clearing-house guarantee funds.

In sum, opportunities should be taken to limit the proliferation of redundant clearing houses and to clear credit derivatives along with interest rate swaps and other types of OTC derivatives.

Clearing would not have prevented the AIG Fiasco

AIG's recent massive losses, covered by large U.S. government bailouts, were the result of immense credit default swap positions, by which AIG FP, a subsidiary of AIG, promised to cover default losses on residential mortgages and other debt instruments with a total principal amount estimated at over $400 billion. The master swap agreements governing these credit default swaps required AIG FP to post additional collateral in the event that its credit rating is downgraded. Because of the immense mark-to-market loss that AIG had incurred on these CDS by this point, it would have been unable to obtain the necessary collateral. As the downgrade became imminent, a large government bailout ensued.

Clearing houses would not have prevented the AIG fiasco. Most of the AIG credit derivatives were customized to specific collateralized debt obligations, and would not have met any reasonable test of standardization, so would not have been cleared. Only better risk management by AIG or better supervisory oversight by its regulators would have prevented the AIG catastrophe, even if clearing houses for credit derivatives had been in place years ago.

Regulation of Default Swaps as Insurance?

Investors are not required to be a lender to the named borrower, or to be otherwise exposed to the borrower's default, in order to buy CDS protection. Both buyers and sellers of protection may use default swaps as a method of speculation over a firm's prospects, just as equity investors are permitted to buy or short sell the firm's equities or equity options. Some have suggested that speculative protection buying should not be allowed, analogous to outlawing the short sale of equities (see, for example, Soros 2009). Eliminating this form of speculation would make CDS markets less liquid. Investors could find it more difficult and more costly to trade; CDS rate quotations would be less reliable as a source of information to investors and others on the prospects of the named borrowers.

Related to suggestions to more tightly regulate the purposes for which CDS protection may be obtained, some have proposed to treat credit default swaps as a legal form of insurance contract, bringing sellers of protection under the regulatory framework of the insurance industry.[1] Unfortunately, insurance is currently regulated within a patchwork of state-level laws and supervision. Until a relatively standard federal or international system of insurance regulation can effectively treat credit default swaps, it seems inadvisable to me to bring credit derivatives into this regulatory framework. If and when that happens, special carve-outs will presumably be needed in order for dealers to make markets effectively, recognizing that the vast majority of dealer positions are offsetting. Clearing will be especially helpful in justifying such exemptions, provided that the clearing house itself is safe and sound.

THE MIGRATION OF CREDIT DERIVATIVES TRADING ONTO EXCHANGES

Although clearing does not require exchange trading, some have suggested that CDS trading should be conducted only on exchanges, which offer clearing as well as superior price transparency. The prices and quantities of each trade would become publicly available. Of course, as usual for exchange trading, the counterparties to trades would remain private, just as they are in the over-the-counter market. The benefits of exchange trading, however, are to be traded against the benefits of innovation and customization that are typical of

---

1. Robert Litan argues that insurers operating across states, as CDS dealers would, should have the option to operate under a new federal insurance regulator, analogous to the optional federal charter system that applies to the banking system (see Litan 2009).

the over-the-counter market. The market for default swaps was built by the dealer banks in the 1990s, at some cost. Now that the CDS market is large and profitable for the dealers, they are naturally reluctant to push trading onto exchanges.

Meanwhile, the relative opaqueness of the OTC market implies that bid-ask spreads are in many cases not being set as competitively as they would be on exchanges. This entails a loss in market efficiency.

The DTCC now provides data on the outstanding amounts of CDS on 1,000 different corporate and sovereign borrowers. Which of these 1,000 types of credit derivatives are ready for exchange trading? Exchange trading is natural for the most actively traded default swaps, such as CDS index products, but we do not have a mechanism in place for the selection and migration of specific types of credit derivatives from the OTC market to exchange trading.

ADDITIONAL PRICE TRANSPARENCY IS POSSIBLE

An intermediate solution may be to add more price transparency to the OTC market with a scheme for reporting the key terms of credit derivatives trades, especially the CDS rate, along the lines of TRACE, a system now used for the post-trade reporting of transaction prices of most over-the-counter corporate and municipal bond trades. Academic research using TRACE data suggests that dealers may exploit market opaqueness when setting bid-ask spreads, and that the dissemination of TRACE data is in some cases responsible for a reduction in bid-ask spreads (see Goldstein *et al.* 2007 and Green et al 2007). Currently, however, credit derivatives are not regulated as securities, which may limit the ability of regulators to require transaction price reporting.

The government could require post-trade price reporting directly from the CDS trading records collected by the DTCC, although this might require new regulations. A case can be made that requiring this additional level of price transparency could actually reduce market liquidity in the less actively traded credit default swaps, if dealer profit margins were as a result reduced to the point that they could not cover their fixed costs for making markets. Another argument against a U.S. regulation requiring post-trade price transparency is the potential migration of CDS trading to jurisdictions that do not apply such a rule.

REFERENCES

Bernanke, Ben (2008), "Financial Regulation and Financial Stability," speech delivered at the Federal Deposit Insurance Corporation's Forum on Mortgage Lending for Low and Moderate Income Households, Arlington, VA, July 8, available at http://www.federalreserve.gov/newsevents/speech/bernanke20080708a.htm.

Duffie, Darrell and Haoxiang Zhu (2009), "Does a Central Clearing Counterparty Reduce Counterparty Risk?" Working Paper, Graduate School of Business, Stanford University.

Goldstein, Michael A., Edith S. Hotchkiss, and Erik R. Sirri, (2007), "Transparency and Liquidity: A Controlled Experiment on Corporate Bonds," *Review of Financial Studies* 20, pp. 235–273.

Green, Richard C., Burton Hollifield, and Norman Schurhoff, (2007), "Financial Intermediation and the Costs of Trading in an Opaque Market," *Review of Financial Studies* 20, pp. 275–314.

Litan, Robert (2009), "Regulating Insurance after the Crisis," *Fixing Finance Series 2009-02*, Washington, DC: Brookings Institution, Mar. 4.

Soros, George (2009), "The Game Changer," *Financial Times*, Jan. 28.

9

Should the Federal Reserve Be a Systemic Stability Regulator?

Andrew Crockett

Introduction

The current financial crisis has revealed the need for fundamental changes in both the content and structure of regulation. As far as the latter is concerned, it has long been recognized that, for largely historical reasons, the United States has an overly fragmented regulatory structure. Organized along functional lines, the U.S. system has two main market regulators (the SEC and CFTC), at least four banking regulators (the Federal Reserve, OCC, FDIC, and OTS), and insurance regulation conducted entirely at the state level.

This fragmentation has generated overlaps in responsibilities, while at the same time allowing important gaps in regulation to

The views expressed are those of the author and not necessarily those of JPMorgan Chase and Co.

arise. Among these gaps is the lack of any agency with overall responsibility for monitoring and addressing systemic risk (a situation that is by no means unique to the United States). This paper considers the need for a systemic stability regulator, what such a regulator should do, and to which agency this responsibility might be assigned. Although many of the observations apply to the specific situation of the United States, much of the argument is of general applicability.

1. WHY IS A SYSTEMIC STABILITY REGULATOR (SSR) NEEDED?

A *first* reason for having an agency with overall stability responsibilities is that consolidation in finance has led to the emergence of a range of institutions that have become so large that their disorderly failure would have major implications for the broader economy. These institutions are not confined to the banking sector, which used to be considered the "core" of the financial system. A half century ago, banks were responsible for 60 percent of the credit extended in the United States. Now, with increased securitization and the larger role of capital markets and institutional investors, that percentage is only about 20 percent. Large non-bank institutions have become of systemic significance.

Second, given the importance of capital markets as a source of funding and vehicle for risk management, the interconnections between financial intermediaries in different sectors have become closer and more complex over time. As we have seen in the current crisis, investment banks, money-market funds, and non-bank institutions such as AIG can generate vulnerabilities that are quickly transmitted to other players including the banking institutions at the center of the system.

Third, in a competitive but regulated environment, new players tend to arise that are largely or wholly outside the regulatory net. In current circumstances, these include money market funds, private pools of capital (hedge funds, private equity), off-balance sheet entities such as structured investment vehicles (SIVs), and so on. Without an agency responsible for overall systemic oversight, there is no structured way in which the need for regulation of these new players can be assessed.

Fourth, there is a category of institutions that may not have significant balance sheets but nevertheless play an important role in the infrastructure of intermediation, through their provision of broking or informational services. These would include mortgage brokers (at the heart of the sub-prime crisis), credit rating agencies, accounting standard setters, and audit firms. All of these played at least some role in the run-up to the crisis, yet they were largely outside the purview of the current network of financial regulation. Payment and settlements systems, too, though generally overseen by central banks, are of vital importance to the stable functioning of the system.

Fifth, without a systemic regulator, the focus of regulation is likely to remain institutional, rather than holistic. The basic philosophy of existing regulation is that by ensuring the sound operation of each individual institution, the health of the overall system will be safeguarded. This pays insufficient attention to market dynamics, and can constitute a fallacy of composition. Apparently prudent behavior by banks or other financial institutions, acting individually, can lead to systemic strains. The most obvious example is when, faced with falling asset prices, a bank attempts to withdraw from risk by liquidating part of its portfolio. This makes sense for a single institution acting in isolation. However, if all follow such a course, the result can be a vicious spiral, leading to a collapse of asset prices. A systemic regulator should take account of market dynamics leading to systemic fragility.

Sixth, and related to the above, it has become clear that the financial system is subject to *procyclicality*, which can be amplified by an institutional focus in supervision. Measures of risk typically fall during an economic upswing, causing financial intermediaries to economize on capital by increasing leverage. This tends to accentuate a boom. Conversely, measures of risk rise in downturns. This promotes deleveraging, discourages lending, and intensifies the drag on the real economy. Again, no individual supervisory agency is charged with identifying and counteracting this tendency.

Seventh, a fragmented supervisory structure fails to assign responsibility for crisis management and resolution. As we have seen, a complex financial crisis can affect virtually all institutions. A consistent and coherent strategy is needed to confront such a crisis satisfactorily, which implies the need to task a particular agency with this overall responsibility.

Eighth, and last, the global nature of financial markets, and the global reach of large financial institutions, implies that national solutions to emerging problems need to be adequately coordinated globally. It would facilitate such an approach if a single systemic regulator in each country was the interface with regulation and supervision elsewhere.

2. What Tasks Should be Assigned to the SSR?

The foregoing analysis suggests, in broad terms, the tasks that could be assigned to an SSR. What follows is not intended to be an exhaustive list, and in places may include responsibilities that could be assigned elsewhere. However, it includes the main functions that could be attributed to such a regulator.

(i) *Supervision.* There is now general agreement that certain financial institutions, by virtue of their size, or interconnectedness with the rest of the financial sector, are of systemic importance. They have the potential to create significant negative externalities if they get into difficulty and are threatened with disruptive failure. It is important for the SSR to be in a position to continuously monitor the health of these institutions, and to assess how their activities are affecting the rest of the financial system. This does not necessarily mean direct supervisory responsibilities. But it would be necessary for the systemic regulator to be confident that it had access to all the information it needed on a sufficiently timely basis. This would obviously be facilitated if the systemic regulator was at least a leading partner in ongoing supervision. The systemic regulator ought also to be able to define (even if not necessarily to publish) the list of institutions judged to be "systemically important."

(ii) *Oversight.* Beyond being able to judge the health of individual key institutions, the SSR should have the responsibility of assessing the significance of developing trends in financial intermediation, and their potential to generate systemic risk. This could include, for example, the role of new players, new instruments, or new business models. (An example from recent experience would be the growth of the "originate to distribute" model, based on increasingly sophisticated asset structurings, and distributed widely to non-bank institutions.) For reasons given above, this assessment of financial trends need not be confined to financial institutions, strictly defined, but could include, e.g., new means of providing information or financial analysis.

(iii) *Rule making.* The SSR needs also to have the capacity to make rules to curb systemic risk. If, for example, the SSR concluded that increasing leverage was undermining the strength of financial institutions, it should be in a position to prescribe actions to limit such leverage. Or, if a new category of institutions was judged to have become systemically significant, the SSR should be able to bring them under the regulatory net. Care would of course have to be exercised in deciding how much rule-making authority should be delegated through primary legislation, but such legislation should be designed in such a way as to limit the scope for a rule-making gap to arise and persist.

(iv) *Enforcement.* Rule making implies enforcement procedures. While these powers need not be given to the SSR, there is some justification for doing so. In the case of systemic financial regulation, it would be important for enforcement powers to be implemented in a timely way. One example is early intervention in cases where a systemically important financial institution faces a significant threat to its viability. Another would be where leverage was increasing across the financial system in a manner judged to be excessive, in which case powers to define and enforce increases in capital requirements might be needed.

(v)   *Monitoring*. Monitoring systemic vulnerabilities springs naturally out of the supervision and oversight role described above. It differs, however, in that it could include specific sources of vulnerability such as the growth of credit concentrations, "crowded trades," excessive maturity transformation, risk-promoting compensation practices, and so on. It is for consideration whether the SSR should be given the authority (or the requirement?) to publish regularly its assessments of such vulnerabilities, and to take action to address them.

(vi)   *Intervention*. It is natural for a systemic regulator to play a central role in the management and resolution of crises which nevertheless occur. Such intervention could (or should?) include the ability to provide liquidity support to solvent but viable institutions. In addition, it could include solvency support to questionably solvent institutions whose failure would have broader economic consequences of a highly negative kind. And the systemic regulator could also be assigned a role in the winding down of failing institutions, whose disruptive disappearance would pose a threat to systemic stability. This would be simplified if the agency concerned had its own resources, but even if it did not, means could be developed (with suitable safeguards) of accessing the borrowing power of the government, or the balance sheet of the central bank. In any event, putting public funds at risk is arguably a responsibility which requires wider political involvement, which is one of the reasons why even independent central banks are in general expected to limit themselves to liquidity support.

(vii) *International cooperation.* If, as seems likely, governments in other jurisdictions establish broadly similar institutional arrangements, in which an official agency is tasked with systemic oversight, the SSR would take the leading role in international cooperation. This is unlikely, for the foreseeable future, to involve ceding national regulatory powers, but it would desirably include the maximum degree of international harmonization in regulating a global industry.

3. WHAT ARE THE OPTIONS FOR A SSR?

There are a number of possible options for assigning systemic oversight responsibilities. The choice will depend to some extent on the range of tasks assigned to a systemic regulator, political considerations, and historical factors. The range of possibilities in the United States seems to be the following:

- *The Fed.* This has had the support of Chairman Barney Frank of the House Financial Services Committee, as well as others. Support for the Fed reflects its historic role in crisis management, as well as the leading role it has taken in the present turbulence. In other jurisdictions, a high-level advisory group headed by Jacques de Larosière has favored a leading role for the European Central Bank in the proposed European Systemic Risk Council.

- *Another existing regulatory authority* (the SEC, U.S. Treasury, FDIC, or other). Although this option cannot be completely excluded, it is hard to see any existing body being appropriate for the regulatory role describe above, or commanding widespread support. (This is not to say that certain specific functions of a systemic regulator, e.g., resolution of failing institutions, might not be carried out by one of these agencies.)

- *A newly created body.* It is conceivable that at least some of the functions of systemic stability regulation could be assigned to a newly created agency. This could be an agency with powers limited to systemic oversight, or one with broader supervisory responsibilities. In those countries that have integrated regulators (e.g., the United Kingdom, Japan, and Germany), the question will arise as to how much systemic oversight, in addition to their current supervisory mandates, they should also be charged with.

- *A "College" of functional regulators.* Another approach would be to create a body that attempted to combine the insights of a variety of regulators with responsibilities for financial sector supervision. In the United States, the membership of such a coordinating group would be similar to that of the President's Working Group, but it could be created as a separate agency, with Board members drawn from existing regulators, but its own executive authority and a separate staff.

In what follows, the focus is on the advantages and drawbacks of the central bank (the Fed) in the role of SSR. A fuller judgment would have to take into account the pros and cons of other options as well, but that is beyond the scope of this paper.

In practice, any decision about the assignment of systemic responsibilities will also reflect a variety of political considerations, as well as judgments about how well the Fed is perceived to have performed in the current crisis. While this is inevitable, it is not necessarily the best basis for judgment. A decision in this respect ought primarily to consider the *externalities* (positive and negative) from combining the SSR function with the Fed's other functions, such as monetary policymaking. I try to follow this approach in the next section.

4. PROS AND CONS OF CHOOSING THE FED

A number of powerful arguments can be advanced in favor of choosing the central bank (in this case the Fed) as SSR. Central banks have had an historic responsibility for financial stability. This was, in fact, the reason for the establishment of the Fed in 1913. The Fed has been at the center of financial crisis management throughout its life and is endowed with the balance sheet to provide liquidity support to banks in temporary difficulties. Moreover, the Fed already oversees bank holding companies, and has a well-qualified and respected staff. The New York Fed, in particular, has a long history of mostly successful involvement in tackling financial crises.

These arguments, although powerful, are essentially "legacy" arguments. They imply that the Fed is better placed, at present, to perform the systemic stability and crisis resolution role than any other agency. They do not address the issue of externalities in combining monetary policy making and financial stability responsibilities. Thus, they do not necessarily imply that it would be the right institution if the regulatory structure could be re-designed more fundamentally. To judge the case for the Fed in this context, it is necessary to look at the case for combining the financial stability role with the Fed's other key responsibility: that of ensuring price stability.

Here, it can be argued that there are important positive externalities from combining the monetary policy and SSR stability roles. As the implementer of monetary policy, the Fed has a continuous interaction with market participants that gives it a window into emerging vulnerabilities, an important attribute for a stability regulator. Conversely, having responsibility for oversight of (at present) bank holding companies, may help the Fed better understand the transmission of monetary policy actions into the real economy.

It is hard for an outsider to judge how strong these external benefits are. They certainly should not be dismissed out of hand. But they did not prevent the build up of vulnerabilities prior to the present crisis. In other jurisdictions where supervision is outside the banking system (e.g., the United Kingdom, Canada, Germany, and others), there is little evidence that the central banks have felt unduly handicapped in their execution of monetary policy by not having a direct supervisory role.

Let us now turn to the case that can be made against giving additional financial system oversight responsibilities to the Fed. Some of these are also "legacy" arguments that should not necessarily be considered conclusive. For example, it can be argued that the Fed is not at present the primary supervisor of a number of systemically significant institutions. This is less true than it was before the failures of Fannie Mae, Freddie Mac, and AIG, and the disappearance of the independent investment bank model. But even if it were an important consideration, it could easily be dealt with by extending the reach of the Fed's direct supervisory role.

Much more important are the possible negative externalities of combining the roles of monetary policy and financial stability, which need to be set against the advantages described above. The two roles, though involving some overlap, can be argued to be rather different. There could therefore be a dilution of focus. Most management theory tends to emphasize the advantages of limited mandate organizations, and central banks cannot automatically be excluded from this generalization.

A slightly different objection is that the combination of the two roles, each of which is by itself of great importance, would concentrate too much power in a single organization. This would have to be justified by a strong presumption of improved efficiency. Even if the concentration of power were accepted, it would invite closer involvement by the political process. Exercise of systemic regulatory powers would be a subject of intense political scrutiny, both in good times, where the authority might be trying to restrain financial innovation, and in crises, when it would be providing discretionary support to particular threatened institutions.

Political scrutiny, in itself, is no bad thing. But there are two risks. One is that it could lead to the politicization of the Fed's monetary policy role, with potential adverse consequences for price stability. The other is that it could undermine the Fed's credibility, by associating it with decisions that were almost bound to be controversial (unwelcome restraint in good times, unpopular "bailing out" in bad times).

Finally, there is risk of a conflict of interest between the two roles the Fed would be assuming. Although it may seem far-fetched, it cannot be completely excluded that the monetary policy needed to preserve price stability runs counter to the desire to help out a particular institution that faces difficulty, and where the supervisor would face criticism of a failure occurred. One does not have to believe the Fed would succumb to this temptation to be concerned about the risks of a public perception that it had.

5. CONCLUDING COMMENT

Although the foregoing discussion has cast some doubt on the case for the Fed as a systemic stability regulator, it is not intended to be a firm conclusion. As already noted, the case for the Fed has to be judged against the alternatives, and this paper has not considered these in sufficient detail. In particular, it is important to know whether a fundamental redesign of the regulatory structure is possible, or if it will be necessary to assign the SSR role to an existing institution. Three other considerations argue against a "rush to judgment."

First, it is highly desirable that the arrangements for an SSR fit in with other reforms being made to the content and structure of regulation. *Second*, though it may seem counter-intuitive, there is no immediate need to hasten the establishment of a new structure. Doing so will not have a material impact on how the present crisis is resolved, and after recent experience, it is highly unlikely that excessive risk-taking will again become a problem in the next several years. (There is of course a case for "not letting a good crisis go to waste," but it seems unlikely that the passage of time for reflection will cause the severity of the crisis to be forgotten.) *Third*, it would be very beneficial if the arrangements under consideration in numerous jurisdictions were as consistent as possible, and not adopted without regard for what is done elsewhere. To paraphrase Einstein, decisions in this area should be made as quickly as possible, but not quicker.

10

SYSTEMIC RISKS AND THE BEAR STEARNS CRISIS

Michael J. Halloran

THIS CHAPTER EXAMINES the need for an improved regulatory regime to reduce the likelihood of crises and thereby the need for intervention by the Federal Reserve and other government agencies. In particular, I argue that the existing regulatory agencies are poorly set up to address systemically important risks emanating from the firms or sectors they regulate. I define systemic risk here as the type of risk that has the potential to adversely affect not only a single firm or sector but the economy as a whole. Using the Bear Stearns crisis as an example, I show that the Securities and Exchange Commission (SEC), which focuses on customer and investor protection, was not adequately equipped to address mounting, systemically important risks in Bear and other investment banks—especially the risk of excessive leverage.

I also consider whether there is a need for a systemic stability regulator (SSR) of the kind examined by Andrew Crockett in this volume. I conclude that there is such need and argue that the SSR should be an overarching agency or council focused specifically on risks of systemic importance. I then discuss how a SSR could help manage risks that the existing agencies are unable to address. I contend that if entrusted with adequate powers, the SSR would contribute to financial stability by directing the SEC and other financial agencies to take appropriate action when it observes risks that could have a material adverse effect on the economy unless addressed.

The Bear Stearns Crisis

The period leading up to the Bear Stearns crisis provides an excellent example of the inadequacy of the existing framework for regulating systemically important risks in the financial sector. This issue should be addressed in light of actual experience at the regulatory level, before and during the period of market and institutional stress. I offer here the experience of a securities regulator prior to and during the collapse of Bear Stearns, and weave that story around my position.

The SEC was the sole regulator of the five big investment bank holding companies (IBHCs)—Morgan Stanley, Merrill Lynch, Lehman Brothers, Goldman Sachs and Bear Stearns. Since 1934, it had been the regulator of the broker-dealer subsidiaries of those companies. It became the regulator for their holding companies after the IBHCs asked the SEC to assume that role in 2004. The reason for that request was that the European regulators said they would regulate the IBHCs in Europe unless they became regulated by a competent U.S. regulator on a consolidated supervised entity (CSE) basis, from the holding company on down. The SEC accepted responsibility, the IBHCs consented to SEC regulation in 2004 (as to Lehman and Bear Stearns in 2005, after the Chairman I served was appointed), and the European regulators recognized that arrangement—an important exercise in "cross-border mutual regulatory recognition" on their part.

Early Warning Signs

By 2006, there were clear signs that risk was accumulating in the mortgage markets and that such risks could affect the large IHBCs. In November 2006, a mortgage delinquency rate chart from the New York Federal Reserve came across my desk. It was a mortgage delinquency rate chart. It showed subprime adjustable rate mortgage defaults at over 10%; fixed rate subprime mortgage defaults at over 5%; and the prime mortgages default rate around where one would expect it—at least based on what I experienced at Bank of America during the 1990s— 0.5%. In my experience at Bank of America during the 1990s, if any portfolio had this big a problem—if it had gone above 5%, let alone 10%—this would have resulted in both management and regulatory action. There would have been a meeting, there would have been a question as to whether new portfolio management should be brought in, and there would have been hedges placed against the portfolio or portfolio dispositions to reduce or eliminate further hemorrhaging.

The problems in mortgage markets continued to worsen. When I was at the Bank of America in the 1990s, our mortgages were generally 80% of the property value, and the down payment was 20%. The monthly payment couldn't go over 30% of the borrower's monthly income, and the value of the property could not be more than 14 times the annual rental value of the property. Aside from all the 95% mortgages to subprime borrowers, the 14 times annual rental value ratio became more than twice that at the top of the mortgage bubble in 2006.

I gathered up the SEC Chief Accountant, who was a former bank regulator, requested permission to open discussions with the Division of Trading and Markets (the Division that regulates brokers and the IBHCs), and showed them the 10% subprime mortgage ARM default rates. We said, "We think we have a problem here, because the IBHCs have a lot of CDOs, SIVs, MBSs and so forth, full of mortgages. We don't know if they have been properly marked to market. Isn't there a risk here?" We were particularly concerned about Bear Stearns.[1] We also asked, "What happens if they (the firms) go down? Will that not affect the market?" We noted that under the Securities Exchange Act of 1934, the SEC is supposed to ensure fair and honest markets.

Permitting Excessive Leverage

While problems grew in the mortgage markets, increasing leverage ratios also came to present added risk to Bear and other IHBCs. Warren Buffett summarized the problem in a lengthy TV interview on March 9, 2009 on CNBC's *Squawk Box*. He argued that: "The biggest reason we're in the mess, you know, is we did leverage up the country and we essentially made a huge bet on housing, but that led to all kinds of other instruments. . . ." (see Buffett 2009). His position is that re-

---

1. The Chief Accountant and I emphasized mounting risks several times over several months with the Division until about September 2007, as we felt that Bear could have raised more capital, disposed of risky assets, and entered into hedge positions. After that point, Bear could not probably have done much about its position other than wait and hope.

laxed monetary policy, while a problem, was not the biggest problem—the biggest problem was lack of control of leverage. I fully agree. Both companies and regulators are responsible for that.

Reporters have said that the SEC allowed the IBHCs to have greater leverage. That was not true at the outset. The IBHCs walked into the SEC with high leverage (i.e., assets divided by tangible common equity), in some cases of over 30:1, which the SEC generally accepted. It is true that the SEC allowed the consolidated holding companies to have greater leverage than it had previously required of their broker-dealer subsidiaries under the SEC's broker minimum net capital rule. It is also true that the SEC allowed the leverage to increase somewhat after it took over regulation of the IBHCs. For example, according to the monthly required balance sheet of Bear as of January 31, 2008, a month and a half before it went down, its total assets were $476 billion and its total stockholders' equity was $12 billion: a leverage ratio of 39.7:1. Goldman Sachs had about $1.2 trillion of assets and $40 billion in equity, a ratio of about 30:1.

A regulatory call to reduce leverage would have been met with outcries from the U.S. investment banking industry, claiming that it would be rendered noncompetitive with its international competitors. For example, a report commissioned by Mayor Michael Bloomberg and Senator Chuck Schumer argued that overregulation hampered the competitiveness of U.S. investment banks (see McKinsey and Company 2007). A commission established by the U.S. Chamber of Commerce came to a similar conclusion (see U.S. Chamber of Commerce 2007). IBHCs were adamant they did not want to be regulated by a banking regulator as bank holding companies, because they were fearful their leverage would be required to be reduced. Compare Bank of America's balance sheet on December 31, 2007: total assets of $1.7 trillion and total stockholders' equity of $146 billion. That is a leverage ratio of 11.6:1.[2]

To convince the SEC to allow them to have such high leverage, investment banks used the "matched book" argument. That argument refers to the matching of incoming repurchase agreements (repos) and other secured financing transactions against outgoing repos and other secured transactions. The balance sheets of Bear Stearns and other IBHCs showed massive repo and swap books, where basically Hedge Fund A repos (sells) securities to Bear with an agreement to buy them back in a certain time (repo A). This is really a form of secured funding. Then Bear would repo the securities at a higher spread to Fidelity (repo B), in effect making a secured loan from Fidelity. Those secured loans were not included in the calculation of leverage and capital adequacy by the SEC,

---

2. SEC officials have often said the IBHCs could have revoked the consents to regulation, which made the SEC an ineffective regulator. I do not believe that to be true for three reasons. First, the IBHCs rendered themselves subject to the SEC rules, and the SEC could have amended those rules at any time to prevent withdrawal from regulation, or to prevent withdrawal if the SEC perceived material risks in the IBHC enterprise. Second, while SEC rules allowed the regulated entity to give notice of withdrawal, they also allowed the SEC to delay the effectiveness of the notice for an unspecified "longer period of time" (which could be years) if it determined that to be "necessary or appropriate in the public interest or for the protection of investors" (see Appendix E to SEC Rule 15c3-1, promulgated under the Securities Exchange Act of 1934, especially Rule 15c3-1e(a)(10)). Third, if the IBHCs had tried to revoke, particularly during a time of great stress, the SEC could have brought considerable persuasive force to encourage continued regulation under Appendix E.

basically on the theory that repo A was somehow offset by repo B. By eliminating the matched book, leverage ratios were greatly reduced. The SEC accepted the matched book argument. The fly in the ointment was that the repo and other swap funding was short-term funding—the repos were due and had to be rolled over in a matter of days—and in Bear's case, the roll-over period kept getting shorter.

Applying an Inadequate Basel II Framework

Going further with the story, when the SEC accepted jurisdiction over the IBHCs, it adopted Appendix E—an appendix to the broker net capital rule, which was a different net capital rule for the IBHC holding companies, and toward the end it reads just like a bank regulation. Under it, the SEC had the right, once the IBHCs consented to SEC regulation, to require them to modify their internal risk management control procedures, and to be subject "to other conditions necessary or appropriate in the public interest or for the protection of investors."[3] The conditions could be product-specific or category specific—as by requiring the sale or hedging of risky assets, or could simply require an increase in net capital. Did the SEC do or require those things? What it did is actually go in and live with the IBHCs like a bank regulator does, ever more intensely as the stress became greater. But the SEC did not have a systemic macroeconomic risk notion in deciding whether and how much to apply Appendix E conditions. It was not enough.

So what standard did the SEC Division apply for capital adequacy? It applied Basel II, thinking that was the most ad-

---

3. This authority derives from SEC rule 15c3-1(e) under the Securities Exchange Act of 1934.

vanced new bank-like capital adequacy standard. It did the Basel II calculations and mathematically reduced the January 31, 2008 Bear balance sheet, a month and half before it failed, showing assets of $476 billion, to total risk-weighted assets of $120 billion. Much of that was done, as Basel II permits, on the basis of credit agency ratings, which by that time had become suspect on their own. The SEC Division then divided stockholders' equity of roughly $12 billion into the risk-weighted assets figure and arrived at a figure of 10%, suggesting a "well capitalized" bank by Basel II (and Federal Reserve) standards.

The problem with Basel II, aside from the fact it relies on credit ratings, is that it does not really deal with short-term secured funding—it is not in the calculation. Former SEC Chairman David Ruder said: "If there was any fault that could be given to the Commission it was the failure to understand that the risk management in the collateralized debt area was inadequate" (see Scannell 2008). It is something the new systemic regulator should address, because it is that flaw that led to the demise of Bear Stearns. On Friday afternoon March 4, certain institutions decided to stop doing repos with Bear, and then there was a ricochet effect. Bear's $18 billion of liquidity—which was being handed back to customers who requested it, in order to support a solvency appearance—was sent to zero by the next Friday. Repos were "novated" to other institutions (this is an aspect of repos—they and their collateral can be moved to another institution, away from Bear Stearns, by the counterparty). Basel does not pick up on that. What does? The leverage ratio plus proper direct supervision applying bank like standards does. It is likely the IBHCs, now that they are bank holding companies, will have their leverage reduced by the Federal Reserve.

Why was the SEC Poorly Equipped to Head off the Systemic Effects of a Failure of Bear Stearns?

My experience suggests that corporations and agencies work better, work smarter, if they have a single or limited objective to carry out. The SEC is set up to protect consumers and investors, and it performs that limited function well. As the Bear case shows, however, it was not set up to be and was not a very good regulator of systemically important risks in the firms under its purview.

First, the SEC's staff is not trained to perform systemic risk analysis. Staff expertise is concentrated in securities law and disclosure rules, not macroeconomics or systemic financial risk modeling. Second, the staff is busy with individual institutions. It has neither the time nor the macroeconomic information to worry about the big picture.[4] Third, the SEC does not have a clear statutory mandate to regulate systemically important risks. As noted above, the 1934 Exchange Act mandates only that the SEC ensure "fair and honest markets." The SEC staff felt fair and honest markets had to do with protection of investors as opposed to risk reduction across the economy.

In the case of Bear and other IHBCs, the SEC Division acknowledged that it had the power to take regulatory action to "more aggressively prompt CSE firms [including Bear] to take appropriate actions to mitigate those risks."[5] However, the

---

4. Moreover, the SEC only regulated the IBHCs; subprime problems were serious throughout the banking system, the thrifts, hedge funds, the government sponsored enterprises (Fannie Mae, Freddie Mac, and the Federal Housing Administration) and the mortgage bankers, which the SEC did not regulate.

5. See SEC Division of Trading and Markets, Management Response to the Inspector-General's Report on the SEC's Oversight of Bear Stearns dated Sept. 25, 2008, pp. 88-93.

SEC Division did not view it as its mission to use that power to force Bear management to take actions (compare that with the position of the Canadian systemic regulator discussed below). The Division reasoned that: "The Commission's responsibility was not to dictate business strategies to Bear Stearns. Rather it was to…insure that [Bear's exposures] were reported to senior [Bear] management in a manner that accurately reflected the risks."[6] On the question of leverage, it argued that "analysts can easily assess leverage from public financial information."[7] In other words, the Division was focused on disclosure and transparency—the SEC's core objectives—rather than taking direct action to limit systemically important risks.

The SEC Division felt that its primary mission was not to tell IHBCs how to run their businesses. It was to make sure customers of Bear Stearns and other IHBCs—the brokerage account holders—got their money back. And the SEC has stated repeatedly that it is very proud of the fact that no brokerage account customer lost money in any of the brokerage failures.

The Need for a New Systemic Stability Regulator

The Bear Stearns crisis showed me the need to distinguish between generic firm-level risks and those of systemic importance. Free-market principles dictate that regulators should not unduly intervene in the running of businesses. This is a view I share. However, when mismanagement of a business could threaten the broader economy, regulatory measures are required. The

5. *Ibid.*
6. *Ibid.*

Bear Stearns case led me to believe that an agency outside the SEC (and the other financial agencies) needs to be established to focus on systemically important risks and address them—a systemic stability regulator (SSR).

The SSR needs the authority to require the financial agencies to make adjustments in their regulation for the good of the whole economy. The SEC's primary job is protection of investors. The SSR's primary function would be protection of the economy as a whole. The Federal Reserve is focused on monetary policy. The SEC and banking agencies risk weight the asset of and regulate individual institutions—microeconomic if you will. SSR would risk weight and regulate on a macroeconomic basis—for the benefit of the whole economy.

The SSR could not guarantee that systemically important risks are addressed. After all, the UK's Financial Services Authority—which is a kind of SSR—was not able to prevent market turmoil in that country. However, the Canadian experience suggests that an SSR with the right powers and focus can make a positive difference. I attended a speech given on April 18, 2009 at the 2009 spring meeting of the American Bar Association Section of Business Law, by Julie Dickson, the head of the Canada Office of the Superintendent of Financial Institutions (OSFI). She is the primary Canadian regulator and supervisor of federally registered banks, insurance companies and investment banks (provincial institutions comprise a very small part of the overall). She said that their authorizing statute has a clear mandate—it is solvency and economic stability—applied as a cross policy across all institutions they regulate. Not consumer protection, which is left to other agencies. Not monetary policy, which is left to the Bank of Canada. It is safety and soundness. It is risk management processes, and

Canada has not experienced the problems the United States has experienced. She summed it up this way: "we force institutions to take action quite early."

What Form Should the SSR Take?

The SSR should be a new body that can help address problems that the SEC, Fed, and other regulators cannot or do not address, either due to their organizational focus or expertise. Identical systemic regulator legislation has been introduced in the Senate (S.664, Collins) and the House (HR 1754, Castle), calling for the creation of a new Financial Stability Council consisting of all the financial agency heads and one independent chairman. The proposed Financial Stability Council would be able to review, approve, prohibit the issuance of or modify rules and regulations of Federal financial regulators, and insurance regulators, require the issuance of new rules by them, and require them to impose different capital requirements or debt ratios either generally or on particular financial institutions, all for the purpose of monitoring and preventing systemic risk to the financial system of the United States. The Council would have no authority over monetary policy—the Fed would keep that. The Treasury Department has also issued a preliminary proposal. It would go beyond financial institutions and allow the systemic regulator to identify and regulate companies (perhaps including auto companies, mortgage brokers, and the like) based on size of assets, degree of leverage, short-term liquidity (or lack thereof), and the effect on the overall economy if they failed. Additional bills are likely to be introduced soon.

I realize that the Fed and Treasury have the gold—the checkbook to bail out systemically important enterprises— leading some to argue that they should take on the SSR function. However, on balance, I come down in favor of a body like the Financial Stability Council proposed in the Collins legislation, except that I would make a minority of its board members financial agency institution heads and a majority would be independent members nominated by the President and confirmed by the Senate. First, I think monetary policy should be separate, with the Fed. If it is not, I think there would be a risk of politicization of monetary policy if the Fed were also the SSR. For that reason, I believe members of the Council should be given relatively long terms. Second, as stated above, I favor agencies (and companies too) with single missions to accomplish instead of multiple missions. The Financial Stability Council should be entirely focused on monitoring and addressing risks that could affect systemic stability. Third, I believe the purpose of the systemic regulator is to restore and promote confidence—in the market, in the banks, by investors, by lenders, by consumers. Maybe the reason the market has come back from its depths recently is that it is gaining confidence that Congress is going to do something to prevent another crisis. I think that given the less than distinguished record of the existing financial agencies, including the Fed—that could have imposed limits on leverage on financial institutions and the mortgages they originated once it saw the default rates— prior to the present financial crisis, everyone is looking for a new and better solution. The new overarching SSR with rule-making authority would do that. Promoting confidence is the primary goal here.

Necessary Powers for an Effective SSR
An SSR will need real power to be effective. First, I would imbue the systemic regulator with the power to obtain information it needs from companies and regulators, under subpoena

if necessary, like the Collins bill does. It is not enough that there are footnotes in the back of financial statements that list the subprime and Alt-A mortgages and so forth. The key is the *quality of the assets* underlying the CDOs, MBSs, and SIVs. These need to be reported in a comprehensive and detailed way to the systemic regulator for big institutions, and that information should be analyzed by a regulatory body whose sole job is to protect the country from unacceptable systemic risk.

Second, I would grant the systemic regulator power to either regulate the credit rating agencies or to order the SEC to adopt rules to obtain good ratings. The SEC was given regulatory authority over the credit rating agencies effective June 2007, but by that time, all the too-high ratings of subprime instruments were already in. There are at least four problems with the credit rating agencies. The first, and biggest, problem is that they tend not to see far enough ahead based on the trendline information they have available (e.g., the November 2006 default rates on subprime mortgages referred to above). The second problem is a lack of transparency; why don't they post their ratings and then post the aftermarket performance of the obligations they rate? The third problem is that they are paid by the issuers—the very people who want the ratings to be as high as possible. The fourth problem is that they do not do well in adjusting their ratings to reflect reality *after* they make the ratings, because they are not paid to do that: they get all their fees when the rating is made.

All of these problems arise as a result of lack of competition in the industry, something Congress recognized in its legislative report when it gave the SEC authority over it. It is hard for the SEC to create new big competitors. Stanford Professor Joe Grundfest came up with a brilliant idea, which he proposed to the SEC at a public roundtable on April 15, 2009, of buyer owned credit rating agencies (BOCRAs), with a legislative or SEC requirement that all ratings have to include one by a BOCRA. The BOCRA would be owned solely by institutions that are buyers of bonds. Grundfest believes the SEC has authority under the new law to require this. The systemic regulator ought to be able to order it. Basel I and II capital adequacy standards for financial institutions rely on those ratings for risk weighting a lot of assets. Financial institutions have depended on such ratings for their investments, now so severely impacted by mark-to-market accounting.

Another thing the systemic regulator should order is amendment of (deletion of) regulatory rules that rely on credit ratings—something the SEC itself proposed during my watch but has not yet adopted. It could also require the SEC to order posting of after-market performance, comparing after-ratings mark-to-market values for securities to the ratings that were given them. I proposed this while at the SEC, but it was not adopted.[8] Paraphrasing Chief Justice Louis Brandeis, as was often done when the Securities Act of 1933 was proposed, "Sunlight is the best disinfectant" (see Brandeis 1914). That principle was the whole basis for the securities laws in 1933 and 1934.

---

8. On February 9, 2009, the SEC adopted a rule requiring the posting on the credit rating agency website of all ratings action information for 10% of its issuer-paid ratings (or paid for by an underwriter or sponsor). SEC Release 34-59342, amendment to Rule 17g-2. On the same day, the SEC proposed to increase the 10% to 100% for ratings made after June 26, 2007, but to require public disclosure a year after the ratings action. SEC Release 34-59343. But neither of these actions require the disclosure of the after-market performance of the obligations rated (e.g., material price drops, defaults, etc.), which could then be compared by securities buyers to the ratings levels and the delayed timing of rating downgrades, if any.

Third, the SSR needs to be able and willing to impose limits on leverage. The SEC, Fed, and other regulators allowed excessive leverage in the lead-up to the crisis, even though they had the legal power to stop it in the institutions they regulated.[9] I did not see any regulators in the 2000s require the banks to go back to 1990s principles. What I saw were a number of guidance memos come out from the regulators.[10] I have a stack of such

---

9. The SEC had the power under Appendix E (see note 5 and accompanying text). The banking agencies had the power explicitly in section 39 of the Federal Deposit Insurance Act, 12 USC §1831p, which authorizes promulgation of regulations or guidelines (the agencies chose the latter) governing credit underwriting, asset quality and other operational standards; and in section 18 of the FDI Act, 12 USC §1828(o), which directs them to adopt uniform regulations prescribing standards for credit secured by liens on interests in real estate. The adopted uniform interagency standard, in Appendix A to subpart D of CFR part 34, essentially punted on 1–4 family home loans by saying only that if the loan-to-value was over 90% "appropriate credit enhancement should be required." In a complete punt to systemic risk, it also said: "Loans sold without recourse to a financially responsible third party" (i.e., the GSEs) did not need to comply with the regulation at all. As to the argument the unregulated mortgage industry is largely responsible for the crisis, regulators had the power under these statutes to cause the banks to cease lending to unregulated lenders who issued unwise mortgages too.

10. See, for example, Federal Reserve Board Supervisory Letter SR 01-4(GEN) on Subprime Lending, January 31, 2001 and Supervisory Letter SR 07-12; Statement on Subprime Mortgage Lending, July 24, 2007; Statement on Subprime Mortgage Lending of Federal Reserve and other financial institution regulatory agencies, June 29, 2007 (this Subprime Statement "encourages" institutions to evaluate the borrower's repayment capacity); and 2006 Interagency Guidance on Nontraditional Mortgage Product Risks (products that allow borrowers to defer payment of principal and sometimes interest, such as payment option ARMs "require extra scrutiny").

guidance memos that say, "Now you guys, you've got to be more careful. You really need to judge your risks better, and you have to watch out for those payment option and other hybrid mortgages." Guidance and "encouragement" weren't enough. There were no rules or policies adopted that placed limits on leverage, which the regulators had the authority to do. An effective SSR needs to require regulators to take steps that are necessary for systemic risk reduction.

Finally, the SSR should have the power to deal with products that can cause systemic instability in the marketplace. For example, it could tell all the regulators and large financial companies to use 80% mortgages and to adopt all of the other sane 1990s mortgage lending policies I described above. An effective SSR could also require regulators like the SEC and Fed to impose margin requirements on derivatives or take other measures to manage risk in large firms and the system as a whole (on the importance of this issue, see Buffett 2009). The Collins/Castle bill does that by authorizing the SSR to require agencies that directly regulate those products to adopt rules (it may only "recommend "rules on "new financial products"). Let us take money market funds (these are not "new" products). Those funds caused a substantial systemic problem when the Reserve Primary Fund—a large institutional money-market mutual fund—"broke the buck" following the Lehman bankruptcy as a result of its investments in Lehman obligations, resulting in a "temporary" government guarantee of money market funds, which has just been extended to September 2009 (see U.S. Treasury Department 2009). The Treasury Secretary has called on the SEC to adopt rules that reduce the credit and liquidity risk profile of money market funds so that a government guarantee would not be required in the future. The systemic stability regulator could require that such rules be adopted, or it could require funds with riskier investments to be guaranteed by a well capitalized sponsor (see Buffett 2009).

Addressing "Too Big to Fail"

I would not imbue the systemic regulator or any other agency with the power to break up companies on the grounds that they are too big. It is too easy to say: "If you are too big to fail, you are too big." Antitrust authorities will indeed address getting too big by acquisition or by unlawful market practices. But if you are big because you played by the antitrust rules, the fact is that in the global economy we may well need you—to finance the building of the infrastructure we need, to build the big projects throughout the world—and while you do that you will need to spread your risk across a diverse portfolio of businesses and assets, and combine synergies between them. I remember we financed some of those projects at Bank of America. Again, the answer to me to the too bigness issue is: an appropriate systemic regulator to regulate the "too big" so their failure does not damage the economy, and a properly revised bankruptcy law as discussed elsewhere in this volume.

Conclusion

The SSR needs to be able to take a holistic macroeconomic view of the economy and its component big companies and parts, and have that as its full time job. It can look at overconcentration of leveraged assets in certain categories. It can look at over-utilization of short-term funding to invest in long-term assets. It can look at rules or the absence of rules that actually impede financial industry competition. I believe that such a reform can go a long way to restoring market confidence.

REFERENCES

Brandeis, Louis D. (1914), *Other People's Money and How Bankers Use it*, New York, Frederick A. Stokes Publishers, p. 92.

Buffett, Warren (2009), Interview on CNBC's *Squawk Box* Program, Mar. 9, transcript available at www.cnbc.com/id/29595047.

Grundfest, Joseph A. and Eugenia Petrova (2009), "Buyer Owned and Controlled Rating Agencies: A Summary Introduction," Comment Letter for Roundtable on Oversight of Credit Rating Agencies, available at www.sec.gov/comments/4-579/4579-10.pdf.

McKinsey and Company (2007), "Sustaining New York's and the US' Global Financial Services Leadership," Report commissioned by Mayor Michael R. Bloomberg and Charles E. Schumer, available at www.nyc.gov/html/om/pdf/ny_report_final.pdf.

Scannell, Kara (2008), "SEC to Come Under Scrutiny," *The Wall Street Journal*, May 6.

U.S. Chamber of Commerce (2007), "Commission on the Regulation of U.S. Capital Markets in the 21st Century: Report and Recommendations," available at www.capitalmarketscommission.com/portal/capmarkets/default.htm.

U.S. Treasury Department (2009). "Treasury Announced Extension of Temporary Guarantee Program for Money Market Funds, Mar. 31, available at www.ustreas.gov/press/releases/1976.htm.

11

Why and How Resolution Policy Must be Improved

Richard J. Herring

No matter how effective U.S. financial regulatory agencies may be, they will not be able (nor should they try) to prevent all failures of systemically important institutions. The kinds of rigid controls that would be necessary to accomplish such an objective would surely stifle innovation and risk taking to such an extent that they would undermine the static and dynamic efficiency of the financial system. Given that some systemically important institutions will inevitably fail, how should they be resolved? This chapter discusses ways to strengthen resolution mechanisms, which can help reduce the likelihood of crises and the need for dramatic actions like those taken by the Federal Reserve and other agencies during the past 18 months.

TWO UNPALATABLE RESOLUTION APPROACHES: LEHMAN BROTHERS AND AIG

Inadvertently, within two days in September 2008, the United States provided two spectacular lessons in how *not* to resolve systemically important institutions. The first occurred on September 15, 2008, when, after trying to broker a merger of Lehman Brothers (LB) with other, stronger institutions, the U.S. authorities declined to bail it out and sent the holding company, Lehman Brothers Holdings International (LBHI), to the bankruptcy courts for protection under Chapter 11 of the U.S. Bankruptcy Code, the largest bankruptcy in U.S. history. Although LB was by far the smallest and one of the least complex institutions on the list of Large Complex Financial Institutions (LCFIs) maintained by the Bank of England and the International Monetary Fund, it was nonetheless of sufficient systemic importance that its collapse led to substantial disturbances on global capital markets. Credit risk spreads rose to record highs, equity prices fell by 4% worldwide when the bankruptcy was announced and government bond yields declined sharply as foreign exchange carry trades were unwound.

Lehman's total reported assets were roughly $700 billion. Its corporate structure included 433 subsidiaries in 20 countries.[1] This international corporate complexity greatly impeded the orderly resolution of the firm and created significant spillovers to other institutions and markets.

One of the major concerns was that LB was the sixth largest counterparty in over-the-counter derivatives markets. But back offices of other firms succeeded in processing billions of dollars

---

1. Based on Lehman Brothers' 2007 annual report.

of contracts and the International Swap Dealers Association organized an auction to determine settlement prices. Because derivatives contracts in which LB was a counterparty were usually marked to market daily and collateral was adjusted each evening to reflect changes in market prices, losses were relatively light. Losses were much greater, however, with regard to credit default swap contracts written on LB. Those selling protection on LB are in a similar position to bondholders and received a similar price: sellers lost $8.625 per $100 of coverage. A second major concern was LB's key role in the Repo market, which totals roughly $11 trillion and is the short-term, collateralized lending market that banks, broker/dealers, and hedge funds use to finance securities positions. The Fed attempted to address the risk that the market would seize up by allowing broader use of the Primary Dealer Credit Facility through expanding the list of eligible securities. In addition a group of global banks announced plans to use their own capital to establish a $70 billion private sector credit facility for those securities not eligible for the Fed facility. The Fed also announced an increase in its Treasury Securities Lending Facility to $200 billion.

What turned out to be more disruptive were the traditional exposures to LB's outstanding debt. Among the largest unsecured creditors were the U.S. federal government's Pension Benefit Guaranty Corp. and the German government's deposit-insurance arm (McCracken 2008) and money market mutual funds. The latter proved to be one of the most important channels of contagion. One of the oldest money market funds, the Reserve Primary Fund, was forced to write off $785 million of short and medium-term notes and became the first money market mutual fund to "break the buck" in 14 years. This triggered $184 billion in money market mutual fund redemptions and forced fund managers to sell assets into illiquid markets. This spilled over into commercial paper markets including not only asset-backed commercial paper, but also non-asset backed commercial paper that had held up reasonably well and was a key means of financing corporations and banks.

The interbank market seized up entirely with the almost complete collapse of confidence in counterparties in money markets. Spreads between LIBOR and the comparable U.S. Treasury rate rose to nearly 450 basis points, more than double the already high spreads that prevailed before the LB bankruptcy. To stem the outflows from money market mutual funds, the Treasury provided guarantees to all shareholders as of September 19, 2008. This led to cries of competitive inequity from the banking industry and a boosting of the deposit insurance ceiling from $100,000 to $250,000.

In addition, failed trades proved particularly disruptive. Prior to LB's bankruptcy, portfolio managers placed thousands of trades with LB's broker dealer (LBI), many of which were subsequently transferred for settlement to LBI affiliates throughout the world. After the bankruptcy, these failed to settle and this has led to civil proceedings on three continents. The U.K. administrator said that about 43,000 trading deals were still "live" in the London subsidiaries alone and would need to be negotiated separately with each counterparty (Hughes 2008b).

But the fundamental problem was that LB was managed as an integrated entity with minimal regard for the legal entities that would need to be taken through the bankruptcy process. LBHI issued the vast majority of unsecured debt and invested the funds in most of its regulated and unregulated subsidiaries. This is a common approach to managing a global corporation, designed to facilitate control over global operations, while reducing funding, capital, and tax costs. LBHI, in effect, served as banker for its affiliates, running a zero balance cash management system. LBHI lent to its operating subsidiaries at the beginning of each day and then swept the cash back to LBHI at the end of each day. The bankruptcy petition was filed before most of the subsidiaries had been funded on September 15 and so most of the cash was tied up in court proceedings in the United States.

Lehman also centralized its information technology so that data for different products and different subsidiaries were comingled. This was an efficient way of running the business as a going concern, but presents an enormous challenge in global bankruptcy proceedings. LB stored data in 26,666 servers, 20,000 of which contained accumulated e-mails, files, voice mail messages, instant messages, and recorded calls. The largest data centers were in New York, London, Tokyo, Hong Kong, and Mumbai. Moreover, LB used approximately 2,700 proprietary, third-party, and off-the-shelf programs, each of which interacted with or created transactions data. The bankruptcy administrators must preserve, extract, store, and analyze data relevant to the entities they are dealing with. This problem was made more difficult by the success of the administrators of LBHI in quickly selling two important entities that were rapidly declining in value because of loss of human capital: its investment banking operations and its asset management business.

Most of the U.S. investment banking operations—the assets, not the legal entities—were sold to Barclays. This necessitated bringing a Securities Investor Protection Corporation (SIPC) proceeding, which put all LBI accounts under the control of the SIPC Trustee and permitted the broker-dealer to be liquidated. Nomura bought most of the investment banking business in Asia and continental Europe, and LB's asset management business was sold in a management buyout. But this meant that the data was owned by Barclays, Nomura, and the now-independent asset management division and so bankruptcy administrators in other countries are dependent on the new owners for access to data to determine the assets and liabilities of each legal entity. The administrator of the four London subsidiaries complained that nine weeks after the bankruptcy, he had yet to receive a confirmation of the assets owned by these subsidiaries.

The U.S. administrators expressed the optimistic view that they would be able to complete the resolution within 18 to 24 months, but the presiding judge reminded the administrator that the biggest impediments to a timely completion of the administration are the timetables of the other insolvency fiduciaries around the world. The administrators in London warned that it may take years for creditors to get some of their money back, noting that they were continuing to work on Enron, which failed seven years ago, which was about one-tenth the size and complexity of Lehman (Hughes 2008a).

The traumatic spillovers from the Lehman bankruptcy led the Group of 7 (G7) Finance Ministers to pledge "to do everything in their power to prevent any more Lehman Brothers-style failures of systemically important financial institutions" (Guha 2008). Observers said that it came close to a G7-wide temporary implicit guarantee for many or all of the liabilities of systemically important financial firms and a complete retreat from market discipline for some of the most systemically important institutions in the world.

Perhaps because of the unexpected magnitude of the spillover effects from the bankruptcy of Lehman Brothers just two days earlier, the U.S. authorities behaved very differently when they were informed that the American International Group (AIG) would have to file for bankruptcy because it would be unable to meet collateral calls in response to the downgrading of its senior debt rating by Moody's. The losses were concentrated in its unregulated financial products unit in London, which had built a huge book of thousands of credit default swaps guaranteeing the creditworthiness of the various tranches of subprime securitizations. AIG had a $1 trillion balance sheet with operations in 130 countries (Geithner 2009).

Within 72 hours the amount of money AIG needed grew from $20 billion to $85 billion (Dash and Sorkin 2008), which revealed an unsettling lack of clarity about AIG's knowledge of its own risk positions. The Federal Reserve provided $85 billion, but losses continued to mount and in November 2008, the Treasury announced a new rescue package that brought the total cost to $150 billion. On March 1, 2009, the federal government agreed to provide an additional $30 billion to AIG and to loosen the terms of prior loans. The government already owned nearly 80% of AIG's holding company as a result of earlier intervention which included a $60 billion loan, a $40 billion purchase of preferred shares, and $50 billion to guarantee the company's toxic assets.

AIG became a target of outrage when it was revealed that in mid-March it had paid $165 million in bonuses, including bonuses to members of the financial products trading unit that had brought the giant insurer to the brink of bankruptcy. Although the U.S. government had a dominant ownership share in the company, it felt powerless to renegotiate contracts.

Although there is some hope that the sale of some of AIG's non-strategic businesses can repay some of the government loans, massive amounts of going concern value have undoubtedly been destroyed and there can be no guarantee that it will not need still more infusions of government funds to stave off bankruptcy. But to date the government has protected all creditors and counterparties at enormous costs to taxpayers.

The inadequacy of resolution tools for dealing with systemically important non-bank financial institutions leaves society hostage to the success with which these institutions control and manage their risks. When they stumble, society is currently left with little choice but to subsidize them, thus encouraging moral hazard and increasing the likelihood of even larger crises in the future.

THE U.S. SPECIAL RESOLUTION APPROACH FOR BANKS

The irony is that the United States has taken some pride in having developed a superior resolution process for systemically important banks. (Until 2008, the assumption was that banks were the primary—if not only—source of systemic risk.) In 1987, the Federal Deposit Insurance Corporation (FDIC) was given authority to establish a new "bridge bank" to continue some or all of the operations of the failed bank until a final disposition could be made. Under the 1991 FIDICIA reforms, the FDIC was obliged to impose risk-reducing measures on insufficiently capitalized institutions and to take control of institutions when their capital level dropped below two percent. This was accompanied by a least cost requirement, but subject to a systemic risk exception. If the federal financial regulatory authorities agree that the application of the least cost approach would generate systemic risk, the FDIC can choose to establish a bridge bank that continued the bank's systemically important functions while imposing losses on shareholders and some debt holders and repudiating some contracts even if it were not the least cost method of resolution. This approach is intended to minimize spillover costs on the financial system and to provide creditors with an incentive to monitor and discipline banks before the point of failure. The intent is to provide the bank with strong incentives to find a private-sector solution before it reaches insolvency. This legislation has been copied by several other countries.

Unfortunately, it has not been particularly useful in the current crisis for at least three reasons. First, many of the systemically important institutions have taken great pains to avoid being classified and regulated as banks—as for example, Lehman Brothers and AIG. Second, many of the largest banks that have experienced solvency problems have booked 20% to 40% of their assets in their Bank Holding Companies, which are not subject to the FDIC's authority and must be taken through bankruptcy court. This raises many of the issues that were experienced during the bankruptcy of Lehman Brothers. And, third, many of these institutions have acquired hundreds of foreign subsidiaries that would be necessarily be dealt with under local resolution procedures which are often very different than those employed in the United States.

RESOLUTION OBJECTIVES IN GENERAL

Although countries differ with regard to bankruptcy procedures, there appears to be widespread agreement on the goals that such procedures should accomplish. Oliver Hart has identified three goals that all good bankruptcy procedures should meet (Hart 2002, pp. 3–5).[2] First, a good procedure should deliver an *ex post* efficient outcome that maximizes the value of the bankrupt business that can be distributed to stakeholders. Second, a good procedure should promote *ex ante* efficient outcomes by penalizing managers and shareholders adequately in bankruptcy states so that the bonding role of debt is preserved. Third, a good procedure should maintain the absolute priority of claims to protect incentives for senior creditors to lend and to avoid the perverse incentives that may arise if some creditors have a lower priority in bankruptcy states than in normal states. These objectives apply equally to financial as well as non-financial firms. But in the case of systemically important institutions, a fourth objective should be appended: a good bankruptcy procedure also limits the costs of systemic risk. Thus a good bankruptcy procedure for a systemically important financial institution is one that maximizes the *ex post* value of the firm's operations subject to the constraints that management and shareholders are adequately penalized, *ex ante* repayment priorities are retained and systemic costs are appropriately limited.

George Kaufman has proposed a four-part procedure for resolving large, insolvent banks that is largely consistent with these objectives and stresses prompt action because delay may prevent even good bankruptcy procedures from accomplishing the four goals (Kaufman 2004). Insolvency procedures tend to be initiated later than they should be, often after a bank is

---

2. Given that economists do not have a satisfactory theory of why parties cannot design their own bankruptcy procedures, Hart is careful not to describe these procedures as "optimal."

deeply insolvent. Not only does this directly increase the loss to be allocated across creditors, but also this may contribute to an acceleration of losses if the insolvent institution gambles for resurrection. In addition, once initiated, resolution tends to move very slowly. This may further exacerbate losses if assets cannot be adequately safeguarded and actively managed with profit incentives. Moreover, it increases the probability of systemic spillover to the extent that counterparties are unable to clarify and hedge their positions, borrowers are unable to make use of their collateral or draw on outstanding commitments, and depositors lose access to their funds.

Similarly, the international scope of an institution's operations may also impede the effectiveness of good insolvency procedures. The fragmentation of oversight that is inherent in a global network is likely to delay recognition of insolvency, quite apart from the expanded scope that it affords managers to conceal insolvency if they wish to do so. Once insolvency is recognized, moreover, it is much more difficult to institute insolvency proceedings. First is the question of which jurisdiction initiates the proceedings. The jurisdiction in which the bank is chartered? The jurisdiction in which most of the bank's assets are located? The jurisdiction from which the bank is managed? (In many cases, these answers need not be the same.) A related question, since the answer may vary from jurisdiction to jurisdiction, is what entity initiates the insolvency proceedings. The creditors? A bankruptcy court? A regulator? Or the insolvent entity itself?

Moreover, it is quite possible for insolvency proceedings to be initiated more or less simultaneously in several different jurisdictions that have conflicting rules on how the resolution should be conducted including such details as the perfection of collateral, the right of set off (if any), and the recognition of close-out netting. At a minimum, there will be substantial coordination challenges with regard to information sharing, the allocations of business units to legal entities and regulatory domains, procedural differences in the acceptance of claims against the bankruptcy estate, differences in the treatment of custody assets, and differences in repayment priorities such as depositor preference schemes or subrogation rights of the deposit insurer (if any). Even under ideal conditions, the resolution of an international insolvency will incur much heavier transaction costs than the resolution of a purely domestic institution with comparable losses.

What Needs to be Done?

To improve the resolution process, the relevant financial regulators (including, possibly, a Systemic Stability Regulator of the type discussed by Andrew Crockett in this volume) will need examination powers and data to identify and perform diagnosis and triage on all systemically important institutions.[3]

---

3. For reasons of space I will ignore the difficult questions of how systemically important institutions can be identified and whether the identification should be made publicly available. I will also ignore the issue of where the resolution authority should be housed, except to note that it will inevitably have to depend on information gathered by the relevant regulators. If there is a way to hold the same regulators accountable for resolution activity, it could be efficient to do so. Unfortunately, regulators have often displayed a preference to delay resolution until losses have mounted to catastrophic proportions. Because resolution may require funds it will need either a funding base (or perhaps) an *ex post* levy on other systemic institutions or an association with the Treasury or the central bank.

They should separate problem financial institutions from non-problem institutions. Non-problem institutions can be scrutinized less intensively and frequently, but they should not be forgotten since AAA-rated institutions can collapse with alarming speed and in the aggregate create systemic problems. Problem financial institutions require greater scrutiny to be separated into those that are simply weak from those that are probably insolvent. The former should be required to file remediation plans, while the latter will need to be resolved.

One of the most seductive but dangerous approaches at this stage is forbearance. Resolution procedures tend to be initiated long after an institution is insolvent. Bad news is concealed as long as possible. Managers are reluctant to share bad news with their supervisors because they fear loss of discretion for dealing with the problem or that leakage of the information could precipitate a liquidity crisis or that they may simply lose their jobs. It is inherently difficult for an outsider to know the true condition of a systemically important institution. (For example, Morgan Stanley, a firm which specializes in valuing other firms, tried to sell itself to Wachovia two weeks before Wachovia was forced to merge.) Thus, usually problems are discovered with a lag. Supervisors often delay resolving an insolvent institution in the hope that it will bounce back.

Unfortunately, supervisors tend to be judged on failures that occur on their watch, rather than the costs of resource misallocations from letting an insolvent financial institution operate too long. Moreover, they understand that interference with the control rights of shareholders is likely to be challenged. Thus there is a tendency to forbear. But forbearance often leads to larger losses. If the problem is not self-correcting, losses continue, which increases the losses that ultimately must be allocated across creditors or absorbed by the taxpayers. Losses may accelerate if an insolvent financial institution gambles for resurrection, which exacerbates the misallocation of resources and increases the risk of systemic spillovers.

The trigger for instituting resolution procedures varies markedly across countries but there are clear advantages for pre-insolvency triggers for escalating regulatory intervention. They provide a powerful incentive for a financial institution to solve its own problems by either restructuring or recapitalizing or merging with a stronger institution. If it fails to take remedial action, there is a strong presumption that it has negligible franchise value to be preserved. Moreover, if resolution procedures can be initiated before actual insolvency, there will be no losses to be allocated across creditors and thus less risk of systemic spillovers and no need for public subsidies. Pre-insolvency triggers, if well-defined, also remove discretion to forbear from regulatory authorities and help insulate them from political interference.

Probably the favorite resolution technique for most supervisors is to assist in the merger of an insolvent financial institution with a healthy financial institution. This can undermine market discipline, because it almost always results in protection of all creditors, but more seriously, it leads to the creation of still larger systemically important institutions.

The bridge financial institution, not unlike the proposal Secretary Geithner has made to Congress, is probably the most efficient way to deal with an insolvent systemically important institution. But the proposal needs to be specified in much greater detail and should have less scope for supervisory discretion.

The objective should be to make the world safe for the insolvency of any systemically important institution. Part of the answer may be in strengthening the financial infrastructure and making the interconnections among systemically important institutions much more transparent and easier to monitor. But another part of the answer depends on a critical reevaluation of the complexity of tax and financial regulations. On average the 16 LCFIs have nearly 2.5 times as many majority-owned subsidiaries as the 16 largest non-financial firms. Much of this difference is surely a result of attempts to avoid costly taxes and regulations.

As a practical matter, each systemically important institution should be required to file a winding-down plan, approved by its board and its regulators, just as it is currently required to file business continuation plans. These plans should be evaluated critically by the regulators, or in the case of systemically important financial institutions that are internationally active (as most are) by the core college of regulators from each of the countries in which it has important activities. If the winding-down plan does not seem plausible without creating intolerable spillovers, the systemically important institution should be required to take remedial action which may include reducing the number and geographic location of subsidiaries, spinning off lines of business, or downsizing and imposing higher capital or liquidity requirements. Such measures may sacrifice some degree of efficiency,[4] but they will force systemically important firms to internalize some of the costs they now impose

4. Although the vast bulk of empirical research suggests that the productivity cost would be negligible. Economies of scale and scope tend to disappear at $100 billion, a size much smaller than any of the current systemically important institutions. Indeed, the productivity differences among banks at any given scale dwarf economies of scale.

on the rest of the financial system and taxpayers by virtue of their size, international complexity, or interconnectedness.

If this sort of system had been in place for the last few years, would we have had a less disastrous outcome with regard to Lehman Brothers and AIG? It's impossible to know, but one can speculate about this counterfactual. At least three reasons justify some degree of optimism. First, the preparation of a winding-down plan subject to board and regulatory approval might have caused these institutions to grow less rapidly, adopt less internationally complex corporate structures, and engage in less systemically risky activity. Second, the regulator might have been more alerted to the increasing fragility of the financial system and better prepared to forestall or manage the crisis than the currently configured regulatory authorities. Third, if the worst happened, there would be clear plans in place for winding-down an institution in the least disruptive way.

We have learned over the past two years that the cost of letting systemically important institutions jeopardize financial stability when they take excessive risks or make ruinous mistakes is too high for society to accept. As George Shultz pointedly observed at the Hoover Institution's policy workshop on the future of the Fed, "An institution that is too big to fail is simply too big."

REFERENCES

Dash, Eric and Andrew Sorkin (2008), "Throwing a Lifeline to a Troubled Giant," *New York Times*, Sept. 18.

Geithner, Timothy (2009), Written Testimony for a Hearing of the House Financial Services Committee," Mar. 24.

Guha, Krishna (2008), "G7 Pledge 'no more Lehmans'," *Financial Times*, Oct. 12.

Hart, Oliver (2002), "Different Approaches to Bankruptcy," Harvard Institute of Economic Research Discussion Paper no. 1903.

Hughes, Jennifer (2008a), "Lehman highlights need for planning," *Financial Times*, Nov. 7.

Hughes, Jennifer (2008b), "Lehman creditors to face years of waiting," *Financial Times*, Nov. 14.

Kaufman, George (2004), "Depositor Liquidity and Loss-Sharing in Bank Failure Resolutions," *Contemporary Economic Policy*, Apr. 2004.

McCracken, Jeffrey (2008), "Lehman's Chaotic Bankruptcy Filing Destroyed Billions in Value," *Wall Street Journal*, Dec. 29.

KEY PRINCIPLES AND RECOMMENDATIONS

John D. Ciorciari

As THE AUTHORS of this book demonstrate, Federal Reserve actions and interventions associated with the financial crisis carry vital economic and policy implications, both in the short and in the longer terms. Major new programs and facilities raise fundamental questions about the future of the Fed. Will these actions compromise the Fed's independence or lead to inflation? Do recent interventions point toward increased problems of moral hazard down the line? What types of market and regulatory reforms can help pave the way to effective central banking policy in the future? The importance of addressing these questions can hardly be overstated. Independent and effective central banking has provided a foundation for the success of the modern U.S. and global economies, and it must continue to do so.

The authors of this volume present a range of views on the merits and implications of the Fed's recent policy approach. They share, however, the goal of providing constructive analysis that helps the Fed focus on its core mission and exit smoothly from its extraordinary programs. In this chapter, I briefly review some of the major arguments and debates contained in the preceding chapters and draw out key principles and recommendations.

BROAD PRINCIPLES FOR FED POLICY

A major purpose of this book—and the meetings and discussions leading up to its publication—is to identify core principles that should govern the Fed's policy decisions going forward. Some of these principles are specific to the Fed, such as the importance of central bank independence and a credible long-term commitment to monetary policy that promotes a strong economy and price stability. Others are more general in application, such as the need to foresee future ramifications of present policies, to align market players' incentives with socially desired outcomes, and to identify market-based mechanisms to complement regulatory regimes. These principles can serve as guideposts for the Fed and other participants in the process of designing and implementing economic policy.

Weighing Future Consequences
One key principle is the importance of considering the future implications of policy measures taken today. As Donald Kohn explains, the Fed has justified its new programs as necessary responses to a severe crisis and sharp recession. He argues that when the Fed's usual policy tools—the Fed funds rate and ordinary discount window lending—proved inadequate, it had to identify other ways to carry out its mandate. The Fed has thus sought to intervene in broad markets, such as those for

commercial paper and asset-backed securities, where it believes interventions will have broad economic effects.

The authors of this book disagree on the merits of the Fed's argument that it must prioritize "putting out the fire" of current market turmoil, but there is general agreement that the Fed's crisis response has the potential to produce important undesired consequences. Large new lending programs and asset purchases have been financed in large part by creating money in the form of reserve balances at the Fed. This could lead to inflation and compromise the credibility of monetary policy. In addition, the Fed's greatly expanded role in providing credit could lead to inefficient credit allocation and undermine the independence that the Fed has historically fought hard to protect, as political pressure is brought to bear on its lending decisions. George Shultz rightly stresses the political and economic dangers of relying on central banks to finance large government activities during periods of fiscal strain.

Opinions vary on the magnitude of risks presented by the Fed's new activities, which relate to the Fed's capacity and willingness to exit from exceptional current practices, reduce inflation risk, and preserve independence from congressional pressure. Kohn asserts that the Fed is focused on those challenges and has the necessary tools to meet them. James Hamilton and several others express skepticism. Given the dramatic rise in the Fed's reserve balances and unprecedented scope of its activities, their concerns are compelling. It is imperative to keep the intertemporal hazards of current Fed policies in focus.

Putting Incentives First

A second core principle emerging from our discussion is the need to focus on incentives when crafting policies. Misaligned incentives certainly contributed to the current crisis—a point aptly driven home by Allan Meltzer and others in this volume. Government policies promoting home ownership, particularly via off-budget subsidies through Fannie and Freddie, encouraged the overgrowth of the mortgage market and deterioration of loan quality. At the same time, a long period of easy monetary policy gave market players an incentive to "reach for yield" by dealing in assets of dubious quality.

The Fed and other government agencies also contributed to incentive misalignment by allowing banks and financial firms to become "too big (or too interconnected) to fail" without articulating a "lender of last resort" policy. Indeed, the existence of such entities, combined with the absence of a lender of last resort policy, fueled market expectations of a bailout if a major bank or firm were to implode. The result was moral hazard, as anticipation of a government backstop reduced the incentives of market players to manage their risks responsibly.

Marrying Market-Based Mechanisms with Improved Regulation

Responding to the challenges above requires both market-based mechanisms and a stronger regulatory regime involving the Fed and other agencies, at home and abroad. Depending on the central bank for massive bailouts and credit lifelines to vital industries is a perilous way to run an economy. Much stronger support structures are needed to address systemic risks, obviate crises, and reduce the need for costly government intervention. The answer is neither to "leave it all to markets" nor to simply pile on additional regulations, which are often difficult to enforce and relatively easy for market players to end-run. Private and public forces need to work synergistically to achieve optimal growth and stability. This is a third broad principle arising from our discussions.

TRANSLATING PRINCIPLES INTO POLICY RECOMMENDATIONS

In addition to presenting broad principles to help guide the Fed and other relevant actors, the authors of this book attempt to translate those principles into specific policy recommendations. They suggest steps that the Fed can take going forward, as well as ideas on how other aspects of financial markets and regulations can be strengthened to improve stability in the system and make the Fed's job easier.

Steps That the Fed Can Take

The authors of this book present a number of recommendations on steps the Fed can take to maintain price stability, exit from its extraordinary programs, help prevent future crises, and promote market confidence.

Managing Price Stability and Exiting from the Extraordinary Programs

A first set of policy suggestions relates to concerns about inflation and the need for price stability. Kohn argues that the Fed has not found a single monetary policy rule that enables it to address the financial crisis and carry out its dual mandates of price stability and high employment and growth. He also argues that the Fed has the necessary tools to withdraw liquidity and head off inflation. Taylor and others recommend taking a different, rule-based approach to monetary policy. Meltzer argues that guidelines such as the Taylor rule will enhance the Fed's credibility and generate confidence in the markets. During the period of 0 percent interest rates, Taylor recommends that the Fed focus on levels or growth rates in the quantity of a monetary aggregate so as to avoid basing those aggregates on selective credit decisions. To this end, the Federal Open Markets Committee could provide target ranges for the growth of reserve balances, base money, or other aggregates.

To reduce inflationary pressures and avoid inefficient or overly politicized credit allocation, the Fed needs a sound strategy for winding down the exceptional facilities. Some authors have suggested ways of doing so, namely by beginning to terminate programs that are not functioning well or are no longer needed. Withdrawing credit will not be easy. As Peter Fisher argues, the Fed has effectively positioned itself at the center of a new "plumbing system" for credit in the economy. Its new role in credit allocation exposes it to added political pressure, and winding down special Fed facilities will be politically unpopular, especially during a period of relatively high unemployment.

Kohn notes that many of the Fed's new lending programs will need to be terminated once the crisis period ends because the Fed has invoked them as part of its statutory authority to address "unusual and exigent" circumstances. That will naturally reduce the size of the balance sheet. Kohn also notes that the Fed is paying interest on excess reserves and can use transactions such as reverse repurchase agreements to reduce balances. To make it easier to raise rates when necessary, the Fed is also seeking other authority to enable it to absorb reserves.

Other authors of this book express concern about the Fed's ability to unload assets, especially "toxic" ones and securities backed by consumer credit, mortgages, and student and auto loans. Hamilton recommends that the Fed shift toward purchases of quality assets such as long-term Treasury Inflation-

Protected Securities. This, he argues, will help the Fed exit more easily in the future and avoid asset purchases that promote a return to problematic securitization practices.

Taylor likewise advocates focusing on a reduction in reserve balances but challenges the Fed's plans on how to do so. He argues that paying interest on reserves has been ineffective and that other options—such as issuing debt to the public—would jeopardize the Fed's independence and expose it to the credit risks inherent in selective credit allocation. He recommends instead that the Fed undertake a rigorous assessment of the effectiveness of existing facilities and shut down those that are ineffective or no longer necessary. He cites the Term Auction Facility and Fed facility for buying medium-term Treasuries as possible candidates. As this volume suggests, analysts differ on how effective the new facilities have been. Those disagreements suggest the need for urgent further analysis and policy evaluation, both inside and outside the Fed.

Addressing Moral Hazard and "Too Big to Fail"

A third group of recommendations concerns the Fed's ability to help prevent future crises by addressing moral hazard that arises from government guarantees and bailout expectations. Myron Scholes recommends a number of measures the Fed could use to reduce the expected value of central bank guarantees and thereby encourage market participants to manage their risks more effectively. These include using credit default swap (CDS) rates or LIBOR spreads over the Fed funds rate to estimate the premiums the Fed would charge on guarantees; providing guarantees only to investments backed by government debt; and requiring enhanced disclosure of any such guarantees.

The problem of moral hazard is particularly acute for the largest, most systemically vital banks and firms. Several authors of this volume contend that an entity that is "too big to fail" is simply too big and that regulators need to take active measures to prevent banks and firms from overgrowing, such as increasing capital requirements. Not everyone agrees. Michael Halloran argues that large banks and financial firms are sometimes needed to provide functions that smaller institutions cannot. Regardless of how that debate is decided, large and highly interconnected financial entities exist today and are not likely to disappear soon. The Fed and other policy actors need better ways to deal with big, complex financial institutions and the risks to the system that they present.

Meltzer argues forcefully that the Fed must articulate a clear and credible "lender of last resort" policy to avoid the moral hazard that accompanies expectations of a bailout. A clear policy would also help reduce the occurrence of seemingly inconsistent policies, such as the Fed's varying responses to Bear Stearns and Lehman Brothers. Underlying recommendations for clear rules and policies to guide Fed decisions is a key debate evident in this book. To what extent can the Fed be trusted to resist unwarranted intervention and uphold its traditional principles of monetary policy when storms hit? Kohn expresses confidence in the Fed's commitment to sound monetary policy and its capacity to intervene only when appropriate. Other authors of this book are more doubtful and believe that rules can stiffen the resolve of central bankers and help them stick to core principles.

Improving Transparency

Finally, a number of authors point to the need for greater transparency at the Fed. Many of the Fed's recent programs have been designed and implemented with little opportunity for public input and analysis. As Fisher recommends, the Fed needs to articulate clearly what problems it is attempting to address and the means by which it is pursuing its goals. The scale and unprecedented nature of the Fed's recent activities have the potential to generate significant uncertainty in the markets, both about inflation and the Fed's broader role.

Kohn notes that it will be difficult to respond to congressional and public pressure to increase transparency on collateral and counterparties because such disclosure would increase stigma and discourage use of the Fed's new facilities. Nevertheless, there is broad agreement on the merits of improving information flow, toward which the Fed has taken significant steps. It has developed a new website to explain its exceptional programs and balance sheet and has issued public statements with the Treasury about their respective roles. Taylor recommends a series of further steps, including daily dissemination of data on the balance sheet, more detailed minutes of relevant Fed meetings, public release of policy evaluation findings, and clearer statements of key operating policy principles, such as the avoidance of monetization. Transparency and the development of clear, credible exit strategies can help the Fed deal with the intertemporal hazards of its crisis response measures.

Market-Based and Regulatory Reforms

The Fed should not take on too much. Central banks work best when they are able to carry out a limited range of functions within a sound market and regulatory setting. Another priority of this book is to offer recommendations on how market-based mechanisms and regulatory reforms can contribute to a more favorable environment for central banking policy. Better overall management of risk and stability in the financial system can reduce the need for crisis-driven government intervention and enable the Federal Reserve to focus on its core monetary policy mandates. A number of authors draw attention to the need for market and regulatory reform.

Reforming Housing Finance
As noted above, housing policy and practices in the United States misaligned incentives and contributed directly to the financial crisis and recession. Meltzer recommends looking for ways to eliminate the off-budget housing subsidy provided through Fannie and Freddie by subjecting the subsidy to the congressional appropriations process. He also advocates liquidating Fannie and Freddie if politically possible. Fisher recommends consolidating the mortgage guarantee functions at Fannie and Freddie into a single federal mortgage insurer that guarantees only fixed-rate mortgages. These sensible reforms will not be easy to achieve given the powerful political appeal of off-budget subsidies. At a minimum, however, the future stability of U.S. financial markets requires taking a more accountable and responsible approach to housing finance.

Enforcing Sensible Capital Standards
In addition to overinflated housing markets, inadequate risk management in banks and investment banks was another key cause of the crisis. To reduce future vulnerabilities, the capital adequacy framework requires reform. Scholes recommends increasing capital requirements uniformly for financial entities by requiring equity capital sufficient to absorb shocks to each class of that entity's assets. He argues that mark-to-market accounting is sensible but that regulators should be empowered to evaluate capital adequacy using other accounting measures when appropriate. He also suggests a slightly more radical measure: requiring banks to leverage their operations only through convertible debt, which would turn into a predetermined fraction

of equity on the occurrence of a shock or at the direction of the relevant regulator. This, he argues, would help reduce the demand for government bailouts, because banks would not need to engage in fire sales of assets to raise capital in a crisis.

Other authors of this book suggest further areas for improvement. Halloran recommends revising the Basel II framework to take better account of short-term secured funding, which lay at the heart of the Bear Stearns crisis. Fisher recommends refocusing attention on the quality of underwriting of assets, rather than focusing only on crude capital ratios. Meltzer adds that regulators have been lax in applying their legal authority under the Federal Deposit Insurance Improvement Act (FDICIA) to intervene in troubled banks when capital falls below required limits. He recommends extending the provisions of FDICIA to all financial firms. Taken together, the suggestions in this book can be reduced to a simple and sensible formula: capital adequacy standards need to be higher, and regulators need both the will and authority to take actions when deficiencies arise.

Strengthening Rating Agencies
Part of the problem with capital adequacy rules was their reliance on rating agencies, which have been the target of intense criticism during the financial crisis. Improving the accuracy of their assessments is essential. Meltzer recommends adopting a proposal whereby the accuracy of rating agencies' past assessments is reported to the public and influences fees. Halloran recommends implementing a proposal by Joe Grundfest to establish buyer-owned credit rating agencies (BOCRAs) owned by buyers of bonds and requiring all ratings to include at least one by such a BOCRA. He also advocates removing regulatory rules that rely on credit rating agencies and suggests requiring

firms to disclose after-rating performance of particular assets. A common theme underlying these proposals is the need to use market-based disclosure mechanisms to give rating agencies the incentive to do a better job.

Improving the Derivatives Markets

Derivatives markets, which figured prominently in the AIG crisis and contributed to recent market turmoil, also require reform. One issue to address is transparency. Myron Scholes recommends "moving risks to markets" and away from financial institutions, because in transparent and liquid markets (such as those for equity or government bonds), shocks can be more easily absorbed via the changing prices of assets. Conversely, when financial institutions accumulate large volumes of relatively illiquid leveraged assets, they become more vulnerable to shocks and paralysis.

One way to improve price discovery mechanisms and increase resilience to shocks would be to require some credit derivative contracts to migrate from over-the-counter markets onto exchanges. Fisher recommends that any names that can trade both credit default swaps and underlying bonds on an exchange should do so. Duffie advocates a slightly more cautionary approach, arguing that the tremendous diversity of credit derivatives products would make it difficult to decide which ones to move onto exchanges and citing the need to avoid stifling innovation by reducing some of the profitability of new products. He recommends improving price transparency by requiring dealers to report trade prices as they do via the TRACE system for corporate and municipal bonds, though noting certain challenges to implementing such a system.

Highly customized credit derivative contracts raise other issues, because they lack sufficient demand to be traded on exchanges. Fisher recommends regulating such products as insurance contracts and subjecting holders to a requirement of adequate reserves against potential future exposure. Duffie argues that the patchwork nature of state-level insurance regulation would make that inadvisable. He also recommends that parties should be able to use credit derivatives to hedge even if they do not hold the underlying debt, because allowing them to do so adds price transparency and liquidity to the market.

Despite those differences in view, there is general agreement on the importance of managing risk in customized derivatives. Even a more transparent market would not have prevented the AIG crisis, which stemmed from highly exotic, "bespoke" contracts. Scholes and others provide a useful cautionary note: it will be difficult to devise a regulatory office or agency with the sophistication to keep up with the most exotic new derivatives products. Dealers in those contracts must be given powerful incentives to manage their own risks.

A further set of reforms in the derivatives markets relate to reducing counterparty risks. Scholes recommends requiring all dealers and market participants to post initial margin on derivative contracts. He and Duffie also recommend using central clearing counterparties (CCPs) to reduce counterparty risk in derivative markets. However, Duffie warns that CCPs can only be effective if they are few in number, extremely well capitalized, follow high standards for collateral, and designed to net assets across different classes, such as credit default swaps and interest rate swaps. He thus provides an important cautionary note as new CCPs begin to proliferate in the United States, Europe, and elsewhere. Regulators need to avoid "too much of a good thing;" competition among CCPs could lead some to relax their standards for collateral and thus raise risks to the system.

Reforming the Bankruptcy Laws

To reduce counterparty risk problems, the bankruptcy regime needs improvement. Under current law, when a firm declares bankruptcy, many of its existing contracts are essentially frozen, protecting the troubled firm from counterparty claims. Derivatives, swaps, and repurchase agreements are exempted from that treatment, however. That exemption presents a serious problem when a firm (such as Bear Stearns) gets into trouble because counterparties can foreclose on their collateral immediately, possibly wiping out the troubled entity and causing market calamity. To address that problem—and to provide firms with incentives to take market-based measures to reduce counterparty risks—Fisher recommends subordinating the rights of counterparties with net trading exposures to the rights of other creditors. Again, the key to reform is to align market participants' incentives with desired policy outcomes.

Resolving Firms That Fail

Even if the Fed and other regulators do their jobs well, some firms are bound to fail. Better structures need to be in place to manage that contingency. Richard Herring recommends that the relevant financial regulators be given stronger examination powers and more data to perform diagnosis and triage on systemically important institutions. He also advocates developing more credible "preinsolvency triggers" that would enable regulators to address problems before they metastasize and generate large creditor losses and systemic risk. Such triggers would also have the important effect of giving entities incentives to keep their houses in order. Rather than simply assisting larger institutions in buying troubled smaller ones—which contributes to the "too big to fail" problem—he advocates using bridge financial institutions to resolve entities in danger. Further, he suggests simplifying tax and financial regulations to remove incentives for large financial institutions to spawn subsidiaries (which complicate resolution). Lastly, he recommends requiring big banks and firms to file "winding-down plans" for regulators' review and imposing remedial measures on those with insufficient plans. When firms do fail or when a crisis occurs, Scholes suggests convening a group of relevant experts, regulators, and market participants to review lessons learned.

Possible Roles for a Systemic Stability Regulator
Many of the issues discussed above have given rise to proposals for a new systemic stability regulator (SSR). Andrew Crockett lays out a number of reasons why an SSR is needed. He argues that instability can emerge from a variety of institutions, including both regulated and unregulated market players, making it important to have a holistic view of emerging vulnerabilities. Regulation or supervision of individual firms often fails to address risks of a systemic nature. Halloran's experience at the Securities and Exchange Commission during the Bear Stearns crisis leads him to a similar conclusion: that an SSR is needed to address systemically important risks that existing agencies are not well equipped to regulate. Not all analysts are as enthusiastic. Meltzer casts doubt on the ability of regulators to assess risks as effectively as managers who are given proper incentives. This critique notwithstanding, the idea of an SRR is being widely debated and receives due attention in this book.

The first question is what form an SSR (if any) should take. The Fed has been advanced as one possible option given its in-

stitutional competence, its existing regulation of bank holding companies, and its experience in liquidity provision. The
authors of this volume cast doubt on the wisdom of turning the
Fed into an SSR. Crockett, Halloran, and others recommend
keeping monetary policy and systemic regulation separate to
avoid a dilution of focus and reduce the opportunities for
politicization of central banking policy. Halloran recommends
establishing a council that includes long-term members and
some heads of relevant regulatory agencies.

The powers and functions of an SSR would also need to be
delineated. Crockett recommends entrusting an SSR with su-
pervising systemically significant institutions; overseeing
trends in financial products or practices with possible systemic
risk implications; establishing new rules of prudential behavior; monitoring systemic vulnerabilities; intervening to provide financial support; and cooperating with counterpart
agencies abroad. Halloran favors granting an SSR the necessary powers to set rules on products or practices that generate
systemic instability, enforce leverage limits, police ratings
agencies, and take certain enforcement actions. The interagency group would determine coverage of particular banks and
financial firms by reference to their size, leverage, short-term
borrowing, and other factors. Scholes suggests that an SSR
should aggregate information from financial firms, play an
information-sharing role, and lead efforts to bring more risk
measures onto income statements and balance sheets.

There are numerous other issues to consider designing an
SSR, such as how to define systemically significant institutions,
when to publicize or act on vulnerabilities, and how to function alongside other regulators, especially across national bor-
ders. An SSR will be no panacea—it will face some of the same

challenges that existing agencies face in identifying risks in complex and evolving markets and taking decisive (and often unpopular) action to deal with them. There are also potential hazards to establishing a new systemic regulator. A poorly designed SSR could exacerbate risk by providing a false sense of security or contributing to expectations that the government will not allow large enterprises to fail. Despite the urgency of resolving the present crisis, discussions on whether and how to create an SSR should not be rushed. Careful deliberation and dialogue is required to reform the existing regulatory regime and align incentives properly.

Looking Ahead

This book has addressed some of the most contentious issues facing the Fed and has presented diverse opinions on the appropriateness of the Fed's recent interventions, the impact of those actions to date, and the risks that they pose. The authors of this volume have also debated the best steps to take going forward. Nevertheless, a few broad principles have emerged that represent the most important shared conclusions of the book. Policymakers inside and outside the Fed need to weigh the future consequences of their actions today, focus on incentives, and pursue broader market and regulatory reforms to pave the way toward financial stability and effective monetary policy as they traverse the road ahead.

ACKNOWLEDGMENTS

THE CHAPTERS IN THIS BOOK are based on presentations the authors made at a workshop entitled "The Future of Central Banking" hosted by the Global Markets Working Group at the Hoover Institution on March 30, 2009. It was the second such workshop hosted by the Working Group; the first was held in the summer of 2008. The Working Group was established soon after the financial crisis began in 2007 to bring policy makers, market experts, and scholars together to address key policy issues facing the United States and global economies. We thank the Hoover Institution for generous financial support of the Working Group and the workshop. We especially thank John Raisian, director of the Hoover Institution, who first suggested that the findings of the workshop be made available quickly to a wider audience in the form of this book. We also thank the participants of the workshop for the valuable ideas they raised in discussion, many of which are reflected in these pages. In addition to the authors of this volume, participants included:

- Philippe Barret
- Gary Becker
- Vineer Bhansali
- Nick Bloom
- Michael Boskin
- Alan Dachs
- Robert Daines
- Jim Dignan
- Frederick Furlong
- Joe Grundfest
- John Gunn
- Matthew Gunn
- Michael Halloran
- Tom Hoenig
- Nick Hope
- Chad Jones
- Jeff Jones
- Michael Klausner
- Mordecai Kurz
- Stephen Langlois
- Ed Lazear
- Andrew Levin
- Mickey Levy
- Sergey Lobanov
- Dennis Lockhart
- Jamie McAndrews
- Ronald McKinnon
- George Parker
- Wesley Phoa
- John Powers
- John Raisian
- Michael Rierson
- Ajay Royan
- Martin Schneider
- Kenneth Scott
- John Shoven
- Josie Smith
- Richard Sousa
- Johannes Stroebel
- Cliff Tan
- James Van Horne
- John Williams
- Haoxiang Zhu

John Cogan and Peter Robinson offered helpful comments on the book.

We are also indebted to the dedicated staff of the Hoover Institution. Marshall Blanchard, Michele Horaney, LaNor Maune, Jennifer Navarrette, Jennifer Presley, Susan Schendel,

Marie-Christine Slakey, and Ann Wood all provided valued assistance that made this book possible.

In addition, several authors wish to acknowledge people who offered comments on their chapters. *George Shultz* appreciates the comments of Michael Boskin, Matthew Gunn, and Allan Meltzer. *Allan Meltzer* thanks Marvin Goodfriend, Alan Greenspan, Robert Hetzel, and Peter Wallison. *Darrell Duffie* is grateful for conversations with, or comments from, Tobias Adrian, James Aitken, Diplas Athanassios, John Campbell, Yue Chen, Laurent Clerc, John Cochrane, Bill Dudley, Nathaniel Emodi, Peter Fisher, Ken French, Nadine Garrick, Jason Granet, Joe Grundfest, Anil Kashyap, Matthew Leising, Theo Lubke, Robert Litan, Manmohan Singh, Myron Scholes, René Stulz, Todd Sullivan, Christian Upper, Haoxiang Zhu, and Solomon Zirkyev. *Richard Herring* is grateful to Ken Scott for his comments.

ABOUT THE AUTHORS

John D. Ciorciari is an assistant professor at the Gerald R. Ford School of Public Policy at the University of Michigan. He was a 2008–9 National Fellow at the Hoover Institution, where he coordinated the Global Markets Working Group. He previously served as a policy official in the U.S. Treasury Department and attorney at Davis Polk & Wardwell. He holds a J.D. from Harvard Law School and D.Phil. from the University of Oxford.

Andrew Crockett is president of J.P. Morgan Chase International. Between 1994 and 2003, he served as general manager of the Bank for International Settlements. In 1999, he became the first chairman of the Financial Stability Forum. He has also been an executive director of the Bank of England and an official of the International Monetary Fund. He remains a member of the Group of Thirty. He was educated at Queens' College, Cambridge and Yale University and was knighted by Queen Elizabeth II in 2003.

Darrell Duffie is the Dean Witter Distinguished Professor in Finance at the Graduate School of Business, Stanford University. Among other positions, he is the president of the American Finance Association, a fellow of the Econometric Society, a research associate of the National Bureau of Economic Research, a member of Moody's Academic Research Committee, the 2003 IAFE/Sunguard Financial Engineer of the Year, and a fellow of the American Academy of Arts and Sciences. He received his PhD from Stanford in 1984.

Peter R. Fisher is a Managing Director of BlackRock, Inc., and co-head of its Fixed Income Portfolio Management Group. Prior to joining BlackRock in 2004, he served as Under Secretary of the U.S. Treasury for Domestic Finance (2001–3) and at the Federal Reserve Bank of New York (1985–2001). Mr. Fisher earned a B.A. degree in history from Harvard College in 1980 and a J.D. degree from Harvard Law School in 1985.

Michael J. Halloran was the Counsel to the Chairman of the United States Securities and Exchange Commission and Deputy Chief of Staff from 2006 to May 2008. He is the former Group Executive Vice President and General Counsel of Bank of America for several years, in addition to being a partner of Pillsbury Winthrop Shaw Pittman, LLP. He is presently a partner with Kilpatrick Stockton LLP, a national law firm, in their Washington, DC office.

James D. Hamilton is Professor of Economics at the University of California at San Diego. He is the author of *Time Series Analysis*, a best-selling research text on forecasting methods in economics. He has been a research advisor or visiting scholar at the U.S. Federal Reserve Board, as well as the research departments at the Federal Reserve Banks in Richmond, New York, and Atlanta. He received his Ph.D. in economics from the University of California at Berkeley.

Richard J. Herring is the Jacob Safra Professor of International Banking and Professor of Finance at The Wharton School, University of Pennsylvania and Co-Director of The Wharton Financial Institutions Center. Outside the university, he serves as Co-Chair of the U.S. Shadow Financial Regulatory Committee and Executive Director of the Financial Economists Roundtable. He was a member of the Group of Thirty Study Groups on the Reinsurance Industry and on Global Institutions, National Supervision and Systemic Risk. He has also served as a consultant to the IMF, World Bank and various U.S. regulatory agencies.

Donald L. Kohn is Vice-Chairman of the Board of Governors of the Federal Reserve System, where he has been a member of the Board since 2002. Before becoming a member of the Board, he served on its staff as Adviser to the Board for Monetary Policy (2001–2), Secretary of the Federal Open Market Committee (1987–2002), Director of the Division of Monetary Affairs (1987–2001), and Deputy Staff Director for Monetary and Financial Policy (1983–7). He has also held positions in the Board's Division of Research and Statistics and at the Federal Reserve Bank of Kansas City. He is Chairman of the Committee on the Global Financial System, a central bank panel that monitors and examines broad issues related to financial markets and systems. He received a B.A. in economics in 1964 from the College of Wooster and a Ph.D. in economics in 1971 from the University of Michigan.

Allan H. Meltzer is the Allan H. Meltzer Professor of Political Economy at the Tepper School of Business, Carnegie Mellon University and is currently a visiting scholar at the American Enterprise Institute. He is the author of *A History of the Federal Reserve*, a two-volume set covering the years 1913–86. He served in the Treasury Department under President Kennedy and the Council of Economic Advisers under President Reagan. For most of the period between 1973 and 1999, he chaired the Shadow Open Market Committee, a group of economists and bankers that reviewed and assessed U.S. monetary policy. He also chaired the International Financial Institution Advisory Commission in 1998, which provided influential recommendations regarding the IMF and World Bank. He received his A.B. and M.A. degrees from Duke University and his Ph.D. from UCLA.

Myron S. Scholes is Chairman of Platinum Grove Asset Management, an alternative investment fund specializing in liquidity provision services to the global wholesale capital markets. He is also the Frank E. Buck Professor of Finance Emeritus at the Stanford University Graduate School of Business and has served as a professor at MIT and The University of Chicago. He is the co-originator with Fischer Black of the Black-Scholes model, which is used to price stock options, and a hedging technology used around the world to price other option-like claims. For this work, he was awarded the Alfred Nobel Memorial Prize in Economic Sciences in 1997. He has published widely in other areas, including tax policy, liquidity provision, valuation of risky claims, risk/return tradeoffs and risk management. He obtained his Ph.D. from The University of Chicago in 1969. He is on the mutual fund boards at Dimensional Fund Advisors and American Century Mountain View Funds.

George P. Shultz is the Thomas W. and Susan B. Ford Distinguished Fellow at the Hoover Institution. Among many other senior government and private sector roles, he served as Secretary of Labor in 1969 and 1970 as Director of the Office of Management and Budget from 1970 to 1972, and as Secretary of the Treasury from 1972 to 1974. He was sworn in on July 16, 1982, as the sixtieth U.S. Secretary of State and served until January 20, 1989. In January 1989, he rejoined Stanford University as the Jack Steele Parker Professor of International Economics at the Graduate School of Business and as a distinguished fellow at the Hoover Institution.

John B. Taylor is the Bowen H. and Janice Arthur McCoy Senior Fellow at the Hoover Institution and the Mary and Robert Raymond Professor of Economics at Stanford University. Among other roles in public service, he served as a member of the President's Council of Economic Advisors from 1989 to 1991 and as Under Secretary of the Treasury for International Affairs from 2001 to 2005. He is currently a member of the California Governor's Council of Economic Advisors. He received a B.S. in economics summa cum laude from Princeton University in 1968 and a Ph.D. in economics from Stanford University in 1973.

INDEX

Accord of 1951
  debt monetization and, 96–97
  Even Keel and, 6
  Fed/Treasury, 5–6
  history concerning, 5–6, 10
AIG. *See* American International
  Group
Aliber, Robert, 6
Alt-A mortgages, 18–19
American Dream Downpayment
  Act, 17
American International Group
  (AIG), 72
  bailout of, 177–78
  bankruptcy of, 177
  clearing and, 131–32
  lender-of-last-resort policy
    and, 23
  resolution policy concerning,
    177–78, 179
  Appendix E, 157

asset-backed securities. *See* securities, asset-backed
assets
  balance sheet, 68–69, 68f,
    70–71, 71f, 72–73, 73f
  shifting, 41–42

Bagehot, Walter, 23
balance sheet
  assets on, 68–69, 68f, 70–71,
    71f, 72–73, 73f
  currency in circulation and,
    74, 75f
  Guha on, 10
  independence regarding, 79–81
  after LB failure, 71–74, 73f, 75f
  liabilities on, 69–70, 69f, 72f,
    75f
  new philosophy of, 76
  open market operation and,
    67, 75

balance sheet *(continued)*
    price stability regarding, 81–82
    recommendations for, 82
    repos regarding, 67–71, 68f,
        71f
    securitization regarding, 76–79
    transparency regarding, 95, 96
Bank of America, 153–54, 156
Bank of England, 23
bankruptcy
    AIG, 177
    counterparty exposure and,
        37–39, 38n2
    goals regarding, 179–80
    international issues impacting,
        181–82
    law reformation and, 202
    LB, 172, 174–76
    timing regarding, 180–81.
    See also resolution policy
banks
    bridge, 178–79
    capital standards and, 198–99
    convertible debt and, 114–15
    credit underwriting and, 34–35
    crisis blame concerning, 21–22
    FDICIA and, 25
    Fed policy affecting, 58–59
    guarantees regarding, 114–15,
        116
    lender-of-last-resort policy
        and, 22
    recapitalization of, 111–12
    recommendations regarding, 20
    Term Auction Facility for,
        70–71.
    See also Bank of America;
        Bank of England; Federal

Home Loan Banks; Home
    Loan Bank System; invest-
    ment bank holding compa-
    nies; New York Federal
    Reserve Bank
Basel Accords, 26
Basel II, 157–58
Bear Sterns
    Basel II and, 157–58
    debt ratios of, 155
    lender-of-last-resort policy
        and, 22
    leverage damaging, 154–57
    matched book argument by,
        156–57
    mortgage default warnings
        and, 154, 154n1
    repos and, 158
    SEC mission affecting, 159–60
Benston, George, 16
Bernanke, Ben
    on derivatives, 123–24
    Fed independence and, 13
    fire analogy of, 43
    nonbank financial institutions
        and, 64
    on policy targets, 44n3
BOCRAs. *See* buyer owned credit
    rating agencies
bridge bank, 178–79
Buffett, Warren, 154–55
Burns, Arthur, 7
buyer owned credit rating agen-
    cies (BOCRAs), 164–65

Canada Office of the
    Superintendent of Financial
    Institutions (OSFI), 161–62

capitalism, 15–16
CBLI. *See* Consumer and Business Lending Initiative
CDS. *See* credit default swaps
Ciorciari, John, xi
clearing
    AIG and, 131–32
    collateral concerning, 127–28
    compression trades and, 128
    consequences of, 129–31
    default risk regarding, 131
    derivatives markets and, 113–14, 127–32
    DTCC and, 125, 126
    exchange trading and, 133
    netting and, 129–30
    standardization of, 129
collateral, 60–61, 61n3, 127–28
Commercial Paper Lending Facility, 72
Community Reinvestment Act, 17
compensation systems, 27–28, 30
compression trades, 128
conference, Shultz/Aliber, 6–7
Congress
    Fed independence and, 64
    housing subsidies and, 19–20
    lender-of-last-resort policy and, 22, 24
    mortgage warnings to, 19
    TARP influence and, 20
    too big to fail policy and, 24
Connally, John, 7–8
Consumer and Business Lending Initiative (CBLI), 9
contingent capital, 116

core principles. *See* principles, core
counterparty exposure, 37–39, 38n2
CPFF. *See* Federal Reserve's Commercial Paper Funding Facility
credit allocation, 59–61, 61n3
credit default swaps (CDS)
    AIG and, 131–32
    Bernanke on, 123–24
    bifurcation of, 37
    clearing and, 127–28
    compression trades and, 128
    documentation of, 126
    exchange trading and, 133–34
    explained, 124–25
    growth of, 124
    as insurance, 124–25, 132–33, 133n1
    LB regarding, 124–25, 126, 173
    netting and, 130
    New York Fed and, 126–28
    price transparency and, 134–35
    risk mispricing and, 36–37, 37n1
    risk reduction regarding, 125
credit easing, 54–55, 86–87
Crockett, Andrew, x–xi, 203, 204
currency in circulation, 74, 75f

debt
    Bear Sterns and, 155
    convertible, 114–15
    financial crisis regarding, 103
    guarantee, 18, 115
    LB, 173–74

debt *(continued)*
    monetization of, 96–97
    risk/reward and, 104–5
    securitization regarding, 78,
        78f.
    See also leverage
deficits, 4
deflation, 21, 81–82
de-levering
    asset price support for, 42–43
    equity injection for, 40–41
    financial crisis regarding,
        39–40
    lower policy rates for, 40
    shift assets for, 41–42
Department of Housing and
    Urban Development, 18
Depository Trust and Clearing
    Corporation (DTCC), 125,
    126
deregulation, 16
derivatives markets
    Bernanke on, 123–24
    CDSs and, 124–25
    clearing in, 113–14, 127–32
    conclusions surrounding,
        200–201
    electronic exchanges and,
        112–13
    exchange trading and, 133–34
    Fed guarantees and, 116
    LB and, 172–73
    New York Fed and, 126–28
    risk in, 112–14, 116
    strengthening, 112–14,
        200–201
    transparency and, 134–35
Dickson, Julie, 161–62

DTCC. *See* Depository Trust and
    Clearing Corporation
Duffie, Darrell, x, 200–201

employment, 52
Even Keel, 6
exit strategy
    conclusions regarding, 194
    credit facility closures as, 95
    inflation protected securities
        as, 82
    preparing, 93–97
    problems regarding, 46–48
    reserve absorption regarding,
        98–99
    reserve interest rate and, 97–98
    reserve quantity/money growth
        and, 93–95
    reserve reduction as, 90–91
    Taylor rule and, 92
    timing of, 92–93
    transparency regarding, 95–97

FDIC. *See* Federal Deposit Insur-
    ance Corporation
FDICIA. *See* Federal Deposit
    Insurance Improvement Act
Federal Deposit Insurance
    Corporation (FDIC), 145,
    178–79
Federal Deposit Insurance
    Improvement Act
    (FDICIA), housing/
    mortgage crisis and, 25
federal funds rate
    Fed policy regarding, 53
    housing/mortgage crisis and, 21
    interest rates and, 58

monetary policy and, 53–54
reduction of, 54, 89–90, 90f
reserve deposits influencing,
89–90, 90f
reserve reductions increasing,
90–91
Federal Home Loan Banks, 19
Federal Housing Administration
(FHA), 17
Federal National Mortgage
Association (FNMA)
debt guarantee and, 18
housing subsidies and, 20
incentives and, 35–36
mandate of, 17–18
mortgage quality and, 19
warnings regarding, 19
Federal Open Market Committee (FMOC), 94
Federal Reserve's Commercial
Paper Funding Facility
(CPFF), 42
FHA. *See* Federal Housing
Administration
financial crisis
adverse feedback creating,
53–54
asset-backed securities and, 56
compensation systems and,
27–28
credit easing and, 54–55
debt reduction regarding, 103
de-levering and, 39–40
GSEs and, 35–36
Meltzer recommendations for,
31–32
monetary policy causing, 34
rating agencies and, 28

regulation regarding, 26–27
responsibility regarding, 31
transparency/risk and, 28–29
two-pronged approach to, 54
uncollateralized lending and,
56–57.
See also housing crisis;
mortgage crisis
Financial Stability Council,
162–63
fire analogies, 43, 105–6
Fisher, Peter, ix, 91, 194, 196–97,
198, 199, 200, 202
FMOC. *See* Federal Open Market Committee
FNMA. *See* Federal National
Mortgage Association
Frank, Barney, 144
Freddie Mac
debt guarantee and, 18
housing subsidies and, 20
incentives and, 35–36
warnings regarding, 19
Friedman, Milton, 6–7

G7. *See* Group of 7
Geithner, Timothy, 9, 184
General Motors Acceptance
Corporation (GMAC),
27
Glass-Steagall prohibition, 16
GMAC. *See* General Motors
Acceptance Corporation
GNMA. *See* Government
National Mortgage
Association
gold window, 8
Goldman Sachs, 155

Government National Mortgage
    Association (GNMA), 18
Government Sponsored
    Enterprises (GSEs), 35–36
Gramlich, Edmund, 19
Great Depression, 16, 47
Greenspan, Alan, 8, 19, 21–22, 24
Greenspan put, 21–22
Group of 7 (G7), 176
Grundfest, Joe, 164–65
GSE. *See* Government Sponsored
    Enterprises
guarantees
    alternatives to, 114–17
    banks and, 114–15
    contingent capital/derivatives
        and, 116
    FNMA/Freddie Mac, 18
    government debt and, 115
    markets and, 110–12, 116
    risk regarding, 110–12, 114–17
Guha, Krishna, 10
guideposts, 6–7

Halloran, Michael, x–xi, 196,
    199, 203, 204
Hamilton, James, ix, 194
Hart, Oliver, 180
Herring, Richard, xi, 202–3
history
    Accord of 1951 in, 5–6, 10
    Even Keel in, 6
    Fed independence and, 4–6
    Fed/Treasury legislation and, 10
    gold window closing in, 8
    lender-of-last-resort policy in,
        22–23
    1970s, 14

Obama administration and,
    8–9
recent, 8–10, 13–16
Shultz/Aliber conference in,
    6–7
in 2008, 14, 15
wage/price controls in, 6–8, 10
after World War II, 4–5
during World War II, 4
History of the Federal Reserve
    (Meltzer), 3–4
    Accord of 1951 and, 5–6
    Even Keel and, 6
    on Fed/Treasury tensions, 5
    after World War II, 4–5
    during World War II, 4
Home Loan Bank System, 17
home ownership, 17–19
housing crisis
    conclusions regarding, 198
    FDICIA and, 25
    Fed blame regarding, 21–22
    monetary policy causing, 34
    risk models and, 29

IBHCs. *See* investment bank
    holding companies
incentives
    as core principle, 191–92
    counterparty exposure and,
        37–39
    GSEs and, 35–36
    Issing Committee on, 29–30
    regulation regarding, 26–27,
        30–31
independence
    Bernanke regarding, 13
    concerns about, 79–81

Congress and, 64
GMAC and, 27
history and, 4–6
hyperinflation regarding, 79–80
politics influencing, 79
reserve absorption affecting, 98–99
taxpayers/risk and, 79, 80
Treasury and, 4–6, 26–27, 64–65
inflation
currency in circulation and, 74, 75f
Fed independence and, 79–80
Fed objectives regarding, 52
interest rates stalling, 62–63
MBS and, 63
Meltzer on, 10
monetary policy and, 62–64
price goals regarding, 63–64
price stability and, 81–82, 193–94
Taylor rule and, 92
World War II and, 4
inflation protected securities.
See securities, inflation protected
innovation, 119–20
insurance, 124–25, 132–33, 133n1.
See also Federal Deposit Insurance Corporation; Federal Deposit Insurance Improvement Act
interconnectedness, 117–19
interest rates, 58, 62–63, 97–98

investment bank holding companies (IBHCs)
Appendix E and, 157
international competition influencing, 155–56
leverage damaging, 154–57
leverage ratios of, 155
matched book argument by, 156–57
mortgage market warnings and, 153–54
regulation revocation by, 156n2
SEC/European regulators and, 152–53
SECs mission affecting, 159–60
Issing, Otmar, 29
Issing Committee, 29–30

Johnson, Lyndon, 6

Kaufman, George, 180
Kohn, Don, ix, 193–94, 197

de Larosière, Jacques, 144
LB. *See* Lehman Brothers
Lehman Brothers (LB)
balance sheet and, 71–74, 73f, 75f
bankruptcy of, 172, 174–76
CDSs and, 124–25, 126, 173
centralization impacting, 174–75
debt of, 173–74
derivatives markets and, 172–73
failed trades and, 174

Lehman Brothers (LB) *(continued)*
  information centralization
    and, 175
  investment banking/asset
    management and, 175–76
  lender-of-last-resort policy
    and, 22–23
  repo market and, 173
  resolution policy concerning,
    172–77, 179
  resolution timetable for,
    176
  SEC and, 152
lender-of-last-resort policy
  consistency in, 24
  Fed regarding, 22, 24, 55
  inconsistency in, 22–23
  as unprecedented, 13, 14
leverage
  Buffett on, 154–55
  excessive, 154–57
  expense of reducing, 106–7
  international competition in-
    fluencing, 155–56
  liquidity and, 107–8
  matched book argument for,
    156–57
  ratios, 155, 156
  as risk factor, 106–8
  SSR limiting, 166, 166n7.
    See also debt
liabilities, balance sheet, 69–70,
  69f, 72f, 75f
liquidity
  policy of, 58–59
  swaps, 70
  volatility and, 107–8
Lo, Andrew, 116–17

Long Term Capital Management
  (LTCM), 21–22
LTCM. *See* Long Term Capital
  Management

markets
  core principle regarding, 192
  Friedman regarding, 6–7
  government influence in,
    118
  guarantees affecting, 110–12,
    116
  interconnectedness in, 117–19
  mortgage, 153–54
  moving risk to, 109–10
  open, 67, 75
  perspective affecting, 117
  review board for, 116–17
  solutions based on, 109–17
  SSR in, 118–19, 139–40.
    See also derivatives markets
Martin, William McChesney, 5
matched book argument,
  156–57
MBS. *See* securities, mortgage-
  backed
McCabe, Thomas, 4
Meltzer, Allan H., viii, 3–4, 196,
  198, 199, 203
  on Fed/Treasury tensions, 5
  on inflation/taxes/controls, 10
  recommendations of, 31–32.
    *See also History of the Federal
    Reserve*
mondustrial policy, 86–87
monetary policy. *See* policy,
  monetary
money markets, 173–74

mortgage crisis
  FDICIA and, 25
  Fed blame regarding, 21–22
  monetary policy causing, 34
  risk models and, 29
  warning signs of, 19, 153–54,
    154n1
mortgage-backed securities. *See*
    securities, mortgage-backed
mortgages
  expansion of, 18
  MBSs and, 57
  quality of, 18–19
  securitization of, 78, 78f
  support for, 17–18.
    See also Federal National
    Mortgage Association;
    Government National
    Mortgage Association

netting, 129–30
New York Federal Reserve Bank,
    126–28

Obama administration, 8–9
open market operation, 67, 75
OSFI. *See* Canada Office of the
    Superintendent of Financial
    Institutions

pipe analogy, 47–48
policy, monetary
  ambiguity in, 43–45
  asset price supports and, 47
  asset-backed securities and,
    56
  consequences of, 190–91
  consistency needed in, 15, 24

credit allocation regarding,
    59–60
credit easing and, 54–55
credit risks and, 60–61, 60n3
as crisis cause, 34
discretion regarding, 14–15
exit problems of, 46–48
Fed assets and, 68–69, 68f,
    70–71, 71f, 72–73, 73f
Fed liabilities and, 69–70, 69f,
    72f, 75f
federal funds rate and, 53–54
flaws in, 14–16, 24–25
inaction regarding, 24–25
inconsistency in, 22–23
inflation regarding, 62–64
intervention quantity
    concerning, 61–62
after LB failure, 71–74, 73f, 75f
lending spreads and, 44
liquidity and, 58–59
mortgage-backed securities
    and, 57
1970s, 14
objectives of, 52
open market operation as, 67,
    75
pipe analogy regarding, 47–48
real rate structure and, 45
repos regarding, 67–71, 68f, 71f
reserves and, 46, 62
Taylor rule regarding, 92
transparency and, 43
in 2008, 14, 15
two-pronged approach of, 54
uncollateralized lending and,
    56–57
unprecedented steps in, 51

Poole, William, 19
PPIP. *See* Public-Private Invest-
    ment Program
price stability, 52, 81–82, 193–94
primary dealers, 55, 55n2
principles, core, 191–92
procyclicality, 140
Public-Private Investment
    Program (PPIP), 42

quantitative easing, 61–62

rating agencies
    buyer owned, 164–65
    improving, 28
    Issing Committee on, 29
    SSR and, 164–65, 165n6
    strengthening, 199
ratings, high, 77–79
Reagan, Ronald, 8
recapitalization, bank, 111–12
regulation
Basel Accords and, 26
    company failure and, 171
    compensation and, 28
    core principle regarding, 192
    Fed role in, 64–65
    good v. bad and, 31
    incentives and, 26–27, 30–31
    international competition
        influencing, 155–56
    leverage ratios and, 155
    lopsided, 34–35
    need for, 151–52, 160–61
    revoking of, 156n2.
    See also deregulation; Securities
        Exchange Commission; sys-
        temic stability regulator(s)

repo. *See* repurchase agreement
repurchase agreement (repo)
    balance sheet and, 67–71, 68f,
        71f
    Bear Sterns demise and, 158
    expansion of, 70, 71f
    Fed assets and, 68–69, 68f,
        70–71, 71f, 73f
    LB regarding, 173
    matched book argument and,
        156–57
    reserve deposits and, 67–68
    volatility of, 68–69
reserve deposits
    absorption of, 98–99
    actual, 88–89, 88f
    currency in circulation and,
        74, 75f
    explosion of, 86–89, 88f
    Fed liabilities and, 69, 69f, 72f,
        75f
    federal funds rate and, 89–91,
        90f
    FMOC regarding, 94
    inflation and, 94–95
    interest rate increase on,
        97–98
    monetary policy regarding, 46,
        62
    9/11 increase in, 86, 88f
    open market operations for,
        67, 75
    projected, 88f, 89
    quantity of, 62, 93–95
    reducing, 90–91
    repos creating, 67–68
    selective credit easing and,
        86–87

Term Auction Facility and, 70–71
resolution policy, 171
  AIG and, 177–78, 179
  for banks, 178–79
  extra issues of, 182n3
  forbearance and, 183–84
  inadequacy of, 178
  international issues impacting, 181–82
  LB and, 172–77, 179
  objectives of, 179–82
  problem/nonproblem institutions and, 182–83
  resolution timing and, 180–81
  triggers regarding, 184
  winding-down plan and, 185–86
risk
  CDSs and, 36–37, 37n1, 125
  clearing and, 131
  collateral and, 60–61, 61n3
  derivatives markets and, 112–14, 116
  false signals creating, 105
  fire analogy regarding, 105–6
  guarantees affecting, 110–12, 114–17
  innovation and, 119–20
  Issing Committee on, 30
  key determinants of, 104–8
  leverage as, 106–8
  lopsided regulation and, 34–35
  market-based solutions to, 109–17
  models, 29
  mortgage markets and, 153
  moving, 109–10
  perspective and, 117
  review board and, 116–17
  reward v., 104–5
  systemic regulator of, 118–19, 139–40
  taxpayer, 60–61, 79, 80
  transparency and, 28–29
  VaR and, 111
  volatility as, 104–6
Ruder, David, 158

saving, 11–12
Scholes, Myron, x, 195, 198, 200, 201, 204
SEC. *See* Securities Exchange Commission
securities, asset-backed
  concerns regarding, 76–79
  financial crisis and, 56
  TALF and, 42, 76–77
securities, inflation protected, 82
securities, mortgage-backed (MBS), 57, 63
securities, Treasury
  Fed assets and, 68–69, 68f, 70–71, 71f, 73–74, 73f
  Fed liabilities and, 69–70, 69f, 72f, 75f
Securities Exchange Commission (SEC), 151
  Appendix E and, 157
  Basel II and, 157–58
  credit ratings and, 164–65, 165n6
  debt ratios allowed by, 155
  IBHCs and, 152–53, 159–60
  leverage regarding, 154–57

Securities Exchange Commission
(SEC) *(continued)*
matched book argument and,
156–57
mission of, 159–60
mortgage default warnings
and, 154
regulation revocation regarding, 156n2
SSR and, 137, 145, 162
securitization
concerns regarding, 76–79
debt regarding, 78, 78f
explained, 77
high rating from, 78–79
as misleading, 79
study on, 77–78
TALF and, 76–77
selective credit easing, 86–87
Shultz, George, viii, 7, 186, 191
Snyder, John, 4–5
Solow, Bob, 6
Sproul, Allan, 5
SSR. *See* systemic stability
regulator
"Steady as You Go" (Shultz), 7
systemic stability regulator(s)
(SSR)
aggregated information and,
118–19
college of, 145
conclusions concerning,
203–5
enforcement by, 142–43
FDIC/SEC/Treasury and, 137,
145, 162
Fed pros/cons regarding, 144,
146–49

financial products regarding,
166–67
Financial Stability Council
and, 162–63
fragmentation and, 137–38
global coordination by, 140,
144
information gathering regarding, 163–64
international cooperation and,
144
intervention by, 143–44
leverage limitations by, 166,
166n7
markets regarding, 118–19,
139–40
monitoring by, 143
negative externalities and,
148–49
new players/information
institutions and, 139
non-bank institutions and, 138
options for, 144–46
OSFI and, 161–62
oversight and, 141–42
positive externalities and, 147
powers of, 163–67
primary function of, 161, 163
procyclicality and, 140
rating agencies and, 164–65,
165n6
reasons for, 138–40
responsibility concerning, 140,
141–44
rule making by, 142
supervision regarding, 141
tasks for, 140–44
timing regarding, 149–50

too big to fail issue and,
167–68

TALF. *See* Term Asset-Backed
Securities Loan Facility
TARP. *See* Troubled Asset Relief
Program
taxpayer, 60–61, 79, 80
Taylor, John, ix, 193–94, 195,
197
Taylor rule, 92
Term Asset-Backed Securities
Loan Facility (TALF), 42,
76–77
Term Auction Facility
banks and, 70–71
closing, 95
credit expansion in, 71–72, 87
rate spikes and, 70
too big to fail, 24, 167–68, 186,
196
trade, 11–12
tranches, 77
transparency, 28–29
balance sheet and, 95, 96
conclusions regarding, 196–97
derivatives price, 134–35
exit strategy and, 95–97
Issing Committee on, 29–30
monetary policy and, 43
suggestions for greater, 96–97
Treasury, U.S.
Accord of 1951 with, 5–6
asset shifting and, 41–42
asset-backed securities and, 56

CBLI and, 9
Fed independence regarding,
4–6, 26–27, 64–65
Fed tensions with, 5
legislation regarding, 10
lender-of-last-resort policy
and, 22–23
SSR and, 137, 145, 162
on TALF, 76–77
TARP use by, 20
World War II and, 4
Treasury securities. *See* securities,
Treasury
Troubled Asset Relief Program
(TARP), 20, 41–42
Truman, Harry, 4

uniform-shock-based-capital
system, 111
unprecedented actions, vii, 13,
14, 51

value-at-risk (VaR), 111
VaR. *See* value-at-risk
volatility
false signals and, 105
fire analogy regarding, 105–6
liquidity and, 107–8
as risk factor, 104–6
risk/reward and, 104–5
Volcker, Paul, 8

wage/price controls, 6–8
winding-down plan, 185–86
World War II, 4

Resolution mechanisms

systemically

foreign exchange carry